5 Lessons Learned
Through Motherhood

What our friends are saying about
5 Lessons Learned Through Motherhood

"The moment I started to read Christina's chapter, I felt completely seen and understood. The way that she shares her real-life lessons of motherhood speaks right to my heart and I have no doubt it will speak to yours. Whether you are a brand new mama or a veteran mom of three (like me!) you will come away from this chapter feeling like you have permission to do motherhood your way. The lessons in this book are universal for moms in all stages. If you haven't learned one of them yet, chances are you will in the future. You will cry, laugh (and probably cry again) but feel so good when you are done. The brutal honesty about the good, bad, and ugly parts of motherhood and womanhood are so refreshing and real. It is so freeing to read about the messy parts of someone else's life that makes you feel more 'normal'. I loved reading this more than I can express and I hope you will too."

— Julia Silvestri Wong

"It takes a great amount of courage to share your story with the world, and even more so when you have carried around a dark cloud of shame for most of your life. A shame that should have never been but something that sometimes society makes us feel... or something that an abuser can also make us feel. Sharing something that has had such a powerful hold on you is tough, and I am sure even scary. However, this, to me, is a great first step in truly healing. By facing your fear head on, your shame head on, and putting a voice to a topic often never spoken about - is brave and for that something to be proud of.

In hearing this story and knowing the person behind it, it breaks my heart but also fills me with so much pride. It takes a lot to recognize, identify and fully embrace the incident in one's life that has catapulted your actions, thoughts and feelings. Where your ability to love and trust must have always been in question. Reading this collection has taught me to never judge a book by its cover. To not pass judgment without knowing someone's back story. It has taught me to protect our children, but also to listen to our children. To create a safe and open environment for all our kids. It has taught me that true love, in the form of a partner, sibling or friend, accepts all... the good, and the work in progress. It has taught me to rely on the community around us and that together, we really can get through anything."

— Sandy Munro

"There's none of the fluffy crap that fills social media. It touches on real situations that happen to almost everyone, but people are often scared to talk about. I teared up reading Darci's chapter because of how true and relatable it is. Thank you for finally saying what needs to be said and bringing these topics to light."

— Kelsey M

"Samantha's chapter was raw and real. It brought up emotions of my own traumatic birth that I still haven't healed. Samantha reignited my confidence in my mama instincts, while also lovingly reminding me that I'm also someone outside of being a mother. A powerful message that I won't forget."

— Sophie Wootton

5 LESSONS LEARNED THROUGH MOTHERHOOD
2021 LeadHer Publishing

Editor - Mary Metcalfe, MS
Cover Design - Christina Williams
Interior Design - Alina Eremenko, Christina Williams
Proofreading - Donna Zuniga

ISBN:

For more information on the publisher, visit lead-her.com
instagram.com/theleadhercollective
admin@lead-her.com

Contents

Contents

INTRODUCTION
Courtney StCroix

Author Photo: Ashley Adams, Flashback Photo Co
Find Courtney: @theleadhercollective

"I don't even really *like* kids." That's what I told myself for most of my life. About half my life, actually, because as I write this, I'm thirty-two years old, and when I was around sixteen, I declared publicly that I probably wasn't going to have kids at all. I'd just finished a co-operative education placement as an eleventh grader at my old elementary school, and whether I was working with kindergarten students or eighth-graders, the verdict was the same: kids are *not* for me. Hell no. Nope. Newwwwp.

It took a conversation with my mom one day, when I was about twenty-three and my sister had just had my first niece, to realize I might change my mind. Somehow, I felt strangely connected to *this* baby. My sister's baby. My niece. What did that mean?

"I didn't really like kids either, you know," my mom told me. "I didn't like other people's kids. But I *obviously* liked my own kids," she said with a smirk and an elbow nudge. "It's different when they're your own. I promise."

I think it's different when they're your nieces, too.

Even though I'd realized in that moment that I was capable of liking "other people's kids" (read: my sister's kid), I didn't start feeling any instinct to be a mother until I was about twenty-five and newly married. In 2013, my sister had just had her second baby, and with my newly acquired double-aunt status, I was all-of-a-sudden thrust into feeling hard the symptoms of baby fever.

Presley was born in November 2015, just after my second niece had turned two.

And I was like... what the fuck?

I was not prepared to feel so unequipped to be a parent. I had a terrible delivery experience and left the hospital feeling under-qualified to be keeping another human being alive. I cried the entire way home. I was bleeding like a faucet (which later revealed a major issue that I had to return to the hospital for two weeks later, but that's a story for another time). My boobs were sore and raw and painful and, like, always "out". My mom could only stay with me for two days, and then my mother-in-law stayed with me for two days, and then on that fifth day? I was alone. And I was terrified.

There's a lot of shit that goes down during that initial motherhood phase, and I of course mean the proverbial shit and also the actual shit that you'll inevitably get on your shirt or your eyebrows or at least all over your hands.

I didn't feel prepared for it, but I did learn from it. I learn from it every day.

My name is Courtney. I'm an author, a publishing coach and mentor, a podcast host and producer, and corporate-climber from the fitness industry turned self-made entrepreneur . . . and these are the five things (so far) that I've learned through motherhood.

1. Motherhood is a seasonal sport.

I know what you're thinking: no, it's not. You don't just get to parent when you "feel like it"; you don't just get to parent during the fall and then take a nice relaxing break during the winter. (Um, wouldn't that be nice, though? Just kidding. Kind of.) What I mean by this is, no matter what "season" you're currently in, it's going to pass. Just like if you hate winter (in Canada) you just have to endure it and suck that shit up for 76 months each year, and then it's over and you can enjoy every other season for one month. Okay, I'm exaggerating. But each stage you go through is truly temporary. One day, you've just returned home from the hospital and you're waiting around for a fresh eight-pound person to take their first poo and inspecting every diaper, pacing around the kitchen table that's full of baby gifts until they do so. And then? Your four-year-old just will *not* stop talking and you start to wonder if you'll ever get to poop by yourself ever again in your entire life.

Each of these things is temporary. Life has seasons, and motherhood has seasons. Each mother is going to find each phase either easy or hard. Your kid is the variable. Got an easy sleeper out of the gate? Then the newborn stage is probably going to be a breeze. Have a kid that simply does not want to potty train? Then you're probably going to loath at least part of that toddler section.

The main thing I've learned and embrace to keep me moving forward? This too shall pass.

2. "Mother" is not the only pair of shoes you should wear.

(The hat metaphor doesn't really work for me, because I rarely, if ever, wear hats. But I have about 23 kajillion pairs of shoes, flip-flops, runners, and UGG boots, so a shoe metaphor makes more sense for me.)

When you become a mom for the first time, it's really easy to sink into that motherhood role and embrace it as your sole duty: to parent another human. It is the number one thing you're responsible for, following their birth, after all. You change your Facebook profile photo to your newborn baby. The only thing you ever talk about with others is what stage or phase or leap your baby is going through. You spend your time browsing Walmart with a sleeping baby in a car seat-stroller combo, and let's be honest, you're mostly browsing through the baby clothes section. You join mom groups and participate in mom-and-baby events so you can get out of the house and meet like-minded people.

And I get all that. I *did* all that. (Except the Facebook profile thing. That still kinda bothers me. You are not defined by the existence of another, just like you aren't defined by any other relationship you're in. You are you, and you're more than someone's mom. Trust me.)

I think somewhere in the first 6–12 months of parenthood, we get truly lost. We may or may not realize it, but there's massive potential for you to become a shell of who you were pre-baby, and to just absorb your role as mother as the sole purpose of your existence. But guess what? You are a mom among other things. Yes, it's a huge part of you now. Rightly so. But, you are probably someone's best friend, a really great colleague or business owner, you're a daughter, a sister, a niece. You're someone who hates country music and loves puzzles, crocheting, and cutting a rug on anybody's wedding dance floor. You're someone who has a passion for painting, singing, writing, or any other creative outlet. You're someone who is either opinionated or agreeable; maybe you're someone's partner; maybe you like pineapple on your pizza. You have many other pairs of shoes to explore than just the sensible motherhood loafers. Just because they may be the ones you wear most often, doesn't mean you should be afraid to bust out some wedges, Converse, Louboutins, or Birkenstocks.

I forgot who I was for a period of new motherhood, and I wish someone had told me that I was still me, even though my main priority at the moment was figuring out how to parent. I wish someone had told me to continue to pursue the things I enjoyed, even though I might have a newborn strapped to my chest. I wish someone had told me to kick off my loafers and go dancing in my wedges, even just every few weeks, so I could sink into remembering who I was and have always been: me.

3. Student and teacher roles are equally important.

As the parent, it's easy to slip into a "my way or the highway" approach to molding your tiny human into the person they're truly meant to be. My daughter has taught me that there are multiple ways to accomplish a single goal. Presley is her own unique being. She sees things through a new, fresh lens, and she pushes back to pressure and time limits, as most young kids do. She is smart and sharp and capable of doing many things on her own, but if it's on someone else's timeline, she resists.

If I approach any situation with her under the pretense that we'll *absolutely* be doing X by Y, she challenges me. In the beginning, I resisted her challenge, and things would get hectic. As I learned to appreciate that she has her own timing in life, I talked less and listened more. I adjusted my expectations. And things then get done even if they aren't done the way I expected. I am not the only one with an opinion or an idea of how we should accomplish our (little, tiny, daily) goals. She has taught me that being the student is as important as being the teacher, and if I can be a great student, I am also a great teacher.

4. You should teach an old dog new tricks.

Sorry, but we're the "old dog" in this scenario. Having a child will probably make you reconsider some of your old "tricks"; your views, values, and perspectives. As you start to navigate, explaining the way the world works to your very curious child, you'll lean on your existing beliefs, but now someone is asking you to explain them, usually by asking "why" 47 times in a row. But where does the person go when they die? How do they get to "heaven"? Why should I be nice to someone who isn't nice to me? Why doesn't Santa just spread out his travel over the whole year? Why can't we move to California? These are silly examples, but when it comes to the real, hard stuff, you have to explain . . . you start to look at it through a new perspective, and I think that's beautiful.

I am grateful for every opportunity to hone my communication skills and clearly explain to my little girl what "boobies" are actually made for, while she's laughing at mine blipping and bobbing around when I'm toweling off after my shower. It's an opportunity for me to adjust my "tricks" and teach myself some new ones. Also, any bad habit you have, your kid is probably going to fucking copy. So, maybe you clean up your language as one of your new "tricks," or *maybe*, like me, you learn how to explain that some words are adult words, and that she's never to say those words because they're only for Mommy to fucking say.

(Just kidding, I don't swear at her directly, obviously. But she's heard me say it regularly, and I've made myself clear: she doesn't say grown-up words, and she doesn't drink mommy's "juice".)

5. Asking for help is not a weakness.

This one took me a long time to understand, especially at the beginning. If you're a new mom, relinquish a little control and ask your mom or dad to watch the baby for an afternoon. Then go do whatever the hell you wanna do, even if that means getting your nails done and then sitting in a park by yourself watching the trees sway back and forth. Your mental health *will* suffer as a new parent. Er, as a parent, just in general. Especially if you're the default parent (and often, moms are the default parent. Not *always*, but often.) *Of course*, your mental health takes a hit as a new parent. You go from **preparing** to be a parent for nine months, galivanting around (somewhat) comfortably, getting the nursery decor sorted, planning baby showers, picking names, and fully functioning as just one person . . . to actually **being** a new parent, responsible for every waking need of *another person*. Not only is this physically demanding work, but it's arguably even more mentally and emotionally draining work.

Your brain is not used to caring for yourself plus one. So naturally, you give up on making yourself a priority. *Don't do that!* Ask someone for help. Once a week, once a month, once in a while... just make sure you ask. Nobody else will understand how you're feeling unless you tell them. You have to be the one responsible for asking, otherwise you'll sit around wondering why nobody notices you're struggling and why nobody has offered to help you. *Woman up and ask for help.* It doesn't make you weak, it helps you fill up your tank and become a stronger woman first, and stronger mom second.

***

Listen, friend. No matter where you are on your parenting journey there are lessons to be learned. If you can look at every difficult moment, every milestone, every celebration, and every challenge as a learning opportunity, you're in for a much more meaningful experience than if you focus solely on the hard parts and spend most of your time wishing for the time to pass more quickly. Motherhood is full of beautiful contrasts. Embrace the highs and lows and take time to reflect on what you learn through every phase.

We're all doing this thing together. (Like, I know we're not *actually* together, but motherhood connects us in a much bigger way than we can even comprehend.) Whether you're reading this while rocking and feeding your 8-week-old at 3:28 a.m., or snuggling into your couch at 8:30 p.m. with three school-aged kids predictably asleep upstairs, I encourage you to embrace the lessons you encounter every day and maybe even take note of them, like all the authors in this collective project have done. What have you learned through motherhood? What parts have been the hardest? What parts have been the easiest? What lessons can you pull from all of them?

I encourage you to put pen to paper and write them down. It's therapeutic, and it helps you see the big picture, whether you're a new-ish mom, or a seasoned grandma. I also encourage you to use the last page of each author's chapter to write down one thing you pulled from their chapter. That's an incredible way to honour another mom's vulnerability and keep something important from each of the 33 contributors' experiences. (It's also a great visual to snap for your IG story... just saying. *wink*)

Solidify your lessons and share them on social media. Tag me **@theleadhercollective** and any of the authors inside these pages. Show us your lessons and let's connect outside of these pages. If you find yourself nodding along or saying "YES, I TOTALLY GET THAT!" during any particular chapter... share that connection with the author in question. She'll love hearing what resonated with you, and it gives us yet another method for connecting further outside these pages.

Now, sit back, relax, and get ready to experience a whole lot of the human connection we're so desperately craving. Mother to mother, we've got this.

Lesson learned.

Sending love always,

Courtney

Founder and Creative Director, LeadHer Publishing

Chapter 1

Andrea Mondoux

Author Photo: Sarazin Photography
Find Andrea: @balanceblissblog

Welcome to the jungle! Motherhood is the one thing we agree to do completely blind, without any idea of what it's actually going to be like, like literally, no idea. I mean, it's not like it comes with a manual! Sure, there are tons of how-to books, but truthfully, I never read any of them (except one which I swear by... ask me about it!)

Throughout this messy journey, I have had so many successes, and I have learned so much. I always knew I wanted to be a mother, but I never imagined the funny, kind, caring, and beautiful little person my daughter could be. It's so incredible to have this person, an extension of the love you and your partner share, and I feel so lucky to have her. But being a parent is also fucking hard. Like countless, *"What the fuck have I gotten myself into?"* moments, and *"Holy hell*, am I even *doing this right*?" It's a wild roller-coaster and there are times where you feel like, maybe, you picked the wrong ride. It's caused me to question myself more times than I ever have, yet it's the most rewarding thing I have ever done. Explain that — right?

Hi there, I am Andrea, and I am so glad to have you here reading these special moments from my journey. In addition to being a mother, I am a Healthy Lifestyle Coach, a podcast host, and a published author committed to changing the way women think about themselves. I inspire and coach women as a career, believe every woman deserves to feel confident and healthy in her own skin, and my daughter was a part of the catalyst for this business. Raising her has changed a lot of things for me along the way, all for the better! I've learned so many things and though the lessons are many, I've chosen to share the most powerful lessons, as well as the things I couldn't have predicted or planned for.

One piece of advice I have for you is that when you feel hopeless, insane, and dark, try and remember that everything is just a phase, and you will get through it.

1. You will never be the same.

When you look into the tiny little eyes of a human you created, everything you think you knew goes out the window. Why? Because holding your child for the first time changes your ENTIRE WORLD, forever. Once that moment happens, you are never the same. You know true love. You become wiser. You know what it's like to be pushed past where you thought you could go, and you survive it. You survive so much more postpartum than you knew you were capable of. You experience tremendous growth. Growth that only comes from choosing someone else, every day, before you choose yourself. Truthfully, it's better on this side.

That doesn't mean you lose who you were before. I am still the same woman I was, but I am an enhanced version, a wiser version. And therefore, I am happily not the same.

2. I love my body as it is.

Before becoming a mom, I had spent years trying to change my body and my negative self-talk. Prior to the day the stick showed up 2–3 weeks pregnant, I had been living a two-year-long weight loss journey of over 50 pounds. I was proud of the work I had accomplished, but in addition to being overjoyed that I was going to be a mom, I was scared about undoing all the hard work I had done and was fearful I would never get to a place where I "loved" my body again.

Now, I am in awe of my body! It created a human! After having been through all the growth of pregnancy and the wild ride that is childbirth, my body continues to show up for me and support me every day. I am grateful for what it has done. The way it stretched and morphed and sustained life. I never imagined the gratitude and acceptance I would learn to have for my body.

3. Your priorities will change – and that's OKAY.

As a social butterfly pre-baby, I was worried that when I had my daughter, I would be held back from my former life. I feared not being able to pick up and go anywhere when I wanted to. I feared missing out on events, trips, and people, because I was "tied down" by a baby and a family.

The day she was born, all of my priorities changed. For the first while, nothing mattered to me as much as she did. Nights felt long, and her being attached to my boobs felt tough. But in hindsight, it flew by. As she started to get a little bit older, I regained some independence and the chance to go out like I used to, but as it turns out, I didn't always want to anymore. I enjoyed being out sometimes, but more often than not, I would opt for being at home with her, with my family, because that's where I wanted to be. I feared missing out on those small moments with them MORE THAN missing out on the trips and the events. And I happily stayed home with them.

4. You will never be ready or prepared! But you figure it out!

I mean sure, we all have our own ideas of what we think it will be like based on the experiences of others. We plan what it's going to be like, but when **push**/surgery comes to shove (see what I did there), all bets are off.

I vividly remember our third day with a baby. My daughter was in the NICU for the first 48 hours of her life. We would go down to visit her for feeds and to spend time with her, but the nurses would encourage us to go back to the room and rest in between feeds. When she was finally discharged to our room, I was elated. It was amazing having her in there with us, showing her off to visitors, and knowing she would be with us all night long. I had spent the last two days with her in the NICU and I thought I was prepared for the first night on our own.

"Thought."

Remember cluster feeding? That night she was up for six hours. She only wanted to be on the boob and since I couldn't get up to grab her, every time she made a peep my husband was responsible for changing her and passing her to me. I remember him saying, in a sleep-deprived state of panic, "How the heck are we going to do this? I can't be getting up all night every night." (Bless him.) It was at that moment I had a shattering thought of, "OMG, maybe we aren't ready for this." I mean, at that point it was too late. But guess what, we figured it out.

And you DO just figure it out. One milestone at a time, one regression at a time. They will all throw you off, just when you think you are in the groove of things, but you always figure it out.

5. Trust the process and give up control.

The first lesson for me came with birth. The way I planned to bring my baby into this world was not how it happened. I needed to be monitored as it was not considered safe for me to go into labor on my own. So, they induced me early. And she arrived early. But she arrived safely. And that was all that mattered.

The way I thought I would be like as a mother, has evolved as it's needed to and that's okay. I have always been someone who likes to control most things in a situation, partially to decrease anxiety around it. Motherhood is not like that. You are no longer in the driver's seat when it comes to plans. I've had to learn to manage my expectations. What I've also learned though, is that it's more important to trust the process, give up control, and know that everything will fall into place as it should.

Key Takeaway

Reflect on this author's work and write down one key idea, concept, or theme that you can take with you in your own life! If something really hit home, connect with the author and get social!

#5lessons #leadherpublishing

Chapter 2

Donna Zuniga

Find Donna: @dee_kay_zee

My first real job was as a lifeguard and swimming instructor during the summer of my junior year of high school. Thinking back, it couldn't have been more appropriate training for motherhood. As mothers, we guard our kids against mental, emotional, and physical harm, while simultaneously loving and guiding them in developing into their truest selves. That's no easy feat! Throughout our motherhood journey, we are — slowly but surely — learning to swim through uncharted waters. Thankfully, we are never alone.

For the next several pages, I get the privilege of serving as one of your navigators. Please understand that I don't take this responsibility lightly. Even though I may not know you personally, I genuinely care about you and your family, and I'm so excited to be a resource for you!

And no matter how you're feeling about this whole motherhood thing, here's the truth: As mothers, we are divinely appointed to raise our children. You are the best mother for your child because — whether biologically, or through foster care, or adoption — the fact remains the same: You were meant for your child, and your child was meant for you. Pretty amazing, huh?

Do we make mistakes along the way? Yep! Plenty of them. We can't learn and become better without first humbling ourselves (over and over again). And so, we wake up each day and we do our best — through the good days and the rough ones, too.

There's a quote from Maya Angelou that has become a sort of mantra for me, and I think it's something that all mothers could use a reminder of: "Do the best you can until you know better. Then when you know better, do better."

Many of the lessons I have learned through motherhood (thus far) stem from teaching myself to ask questions and to open my eyes to potential biases and motives. There are some industries that stand to profit off of inciting fear and doubt in mothers. This is not okay! So, prepare yourself. I am going to write with honesty and passion what I wish someone had said to me while I was pregnant, and in the early years of motherhood — even if my voice shakes.

And just in case you want to know a little more about me before we dive in: I am a wife to my high school sweetheart, a swimmer, a writer, a nature-loving gentle parent of two beautiful, amazing boys, a certified lactation counselor and educator (CLEC), a UCLA alumna, an essential oils educator, and a child of God. Oh, and I don't sugar-coat things. I'm fiercely loyal and will always speak out against injustice, whether I want to or not. I can't help it; it's the lifeguard in me.

My hope for you, in reading my chapter, is that you are inspired to question the narratives we are given daily. I want to empower you to use your voice and your unique gifts — not in an effort to be perfect (none of us are) — but to actively seek to *know better* and *do better* for yourself and your kids, every single day. And when it comes down to it, rest assured, Mama — you were made for this!

1. Trust your gut.

This is a tough thing to explain, but also one of the most important things you can do as a mother. Your motherly instincts are *real*. They are a protective measure and they should not be ignored. The trouble is, a lot of what you will encounter on your pregnancy and motherhood journey will challenge these instincts.

The best way I can describe how to "trust your gut" is to learn to recognize when something seems off. It's when something doesn't sit well with you. Instead of dismissing that feeling or diminishing it as "silly" or an "overreaction" on your part, let it marinate for a little while. It's okay (and actually a good thing!) to dig deeper. It's okay to get a second (or third, or fourth!) opinion.

As women, we have been conditioned in many ways to not question authority figures, to not put up a fight, and to not make a scene. We are "crazy" if we do. But here's the thing: stopping to question something doesn't mean you're nuts; it means you're thorough. It means that you care about making the best possible decision for you and your child.

That nagging feeling that something isn't right is *always* worth your time to explore further.

2. Do your research.

So, what are some of the things that I've found to be worth exploring further? I'll explain a couple of important ones in just a minute, but first I need you to pause briefly, take a deep breath, and open your mind and heart. These are "hot" topics — they shouldn't be, but they are. Please understand that I have absolutely *nothing* to gain from telling you these things (other than to potentially save you from a whole lot of heartache and regret that I have already endured personally).

There are way more than just these that are worth looking into, but the two I'll mention here are the biggies that I wish someone had pointed out to me while I was pregnant, and early on in motherhood.

1. **Read the vaccine insert!** This is not the single 8.5" x 11" paper that the pediatrician hands you as an afterthought when your child receives a vaccine. The actual vaccine insert is included with the vaccine itself that, when unfolded, is probably taller than your child. It goes into detail regarding side effects, post-marketing data, and lists all the ingredients (including adjuvants) in the vaccine. (Hate to break it to you, but it's not just an inactivated virus and saline.) There's also a section (13.1) in every insert that states: "[name of vaccine] has not been evaluated for carcinogenic or mutagenic potential or for impairment of fertility."

I could write a book just on vaccines alone (and maybe I will, someday), but my point here is to implore you to look further; to read the inserts for every vaccine *before* you agree to them for yourself or your child. They can all be found online, or you can request them from the physician. Only *after* reading them, can you truly give informed consent for this medical procedure. I'm not here to judge or to tell you what's right for you and your family, but I am here to say that this is definitely one of those "know better, do better" situations that you should not ignore.

2. Another thing that I agonized over and wish I had researched sooner is **co-sleeping**. Co-sleeping has been done safely and successfully since the beginning of time. When we talk about doing what's "natural" and following our instincts, co-sleeping is right at the top of the list. If it's not for you, that's okay! Remember, my goal here is to empower you to think for yourself and to figure out what's right for *your* individual situation.

For their first year or so, my boys didn't sleep (at all) unless they were touching me, with full access to mama's milk. With my first son, I tried everything *but* co-sleeping for the first six months (and gave myself a wicked case of postpartum anxiety in the process). I agonized over letting him co-sleep because all you ever hear from doctors and the sleep industry is how dangerous it is. And it certainly can be dangerous — like many things — if you don't do your research and take necessary precautions. But once you create a safe sleep environment, co-sleeping can save your sanity and be the biggest blessing — it certainly was for me. Once I let my babies have what they wanted all along, we were all happier because of it.

3. Breastfeeding isn't all or nothing.

Speaking of mama's milk, let's talk breastfeeding for a minute, shall we? As a lactation counselor, I could probably write a book on this topic too, but since I'm limited to this chapter, let's cut to the chase with a few important points:

- You are *not* "spoiling your baby" by breastfeeding on-demand — and that includes breastfeeding your baby to sleep, breastfeeding your baby as soon as they cry, or any other time you and your baby damn well please! In fact, you are answering your child's needs and supporting your milk supply in the process. It's a win-win.

- You are *not* a "bad mother" if you need (or choose) to supplement with formula. I agonized over the decision to supplement with my first son because I thought it would mean that I failed him. On the contrary! It turned out that I wasn't producing enough due to a medical condition that I didn't realize affected my milk supply. This is actually what inspired me to become a lactation educator! The good news is: the vast majority of women are totally capable of exclusively breastfeeding. They just need the support and guidance to do so.

- If you're struggling with breastfeeding, your baby may have a physical or structural issue that is impeding success. Have your little one evaluated by a pediatric dentist or IBCLC to see if a lip and/or tongue-tie may be the cause.

- Watch videos on YouTube on proper breastfeeding latch (including the "Deep Latch Technique" … just be careful that you don't stumble across something that's R-rated. Ha!)
- Whoever said, "Don't cry over spilled milk" has obviously never pumped before. Cry all you want, sweet Mama! They don't call it "liquid gold" for nothing!

And ultimately, when it comes down to it, breastfeeding *isn't* all or nothing. One year, one month, heck, even *one day* (seriously!) is better than nothing at all. Do the best you can, don't be afraid to ask for help, and find resources in your community for extra support (like La Leche League). Breastfeeding — like raising a child — takes a village, especially the first time around!

4. Find your village.

Another major lesson I've learned is to not discredit the importance of finding *your people*. Whether you call them your "tribe" or your "village" or simply your "mama friends" — the goal here is the same: find other women who will lift you up, commiserate with you, tell you that you're an amazing mother (because you are!), and love on you and your kids.

Your partner should be your main supporter, but even if they aren't or if you're going at this whole motherhood thing alone, please know that there are people all around you who want to see you happy and successful. You just have to find them!

Now the hard part: how do you find them? Well, you can join Facebook groups in your area, or you can attend one of the La Leche League meetings I mentioned. You can also follow people on Instagram in the same season of life as you and reach out to them! I can't tell you how many friends I've made from simply direct messaging people on Instagram — and most were complete strangers at first! Don't be afraid of coming off as weird or desperate. Chances are you're already weird (ha!) and that other mama might be desperate for someone to talk to (or to text while hiding in the bathroom). And if you are having trouble or feel alone, please tell someone. Don't hold it all inside and suffer! Tomorrow is a new day and your kiddos are counting on you!

5. Proof of Mama,

Speaking of YOU, I'm sure many of the other amazing authors in this book will tell you some version of "don't forget about *you*" — and they aren't wrong! You matter, Mama! But I'm going to take it one step further and tell you not to forget about taking some *photos* with you in them, too!

Thanks to smartphones, you will literally take thousands of photos of your children; but what about you, Mom? Don't be like me with my first child and think that you have to "just lose a few more pounds" or "put a little makeup on" before you can get in the photo with your kid. (And then you don't get around to doing either and are left out.)

It's okay if you don't look or feel like you did before kids because guess what, Mama? When that baby of yours was born, you were born again, too! You're a whole new person now, and everything will work itself out just as it should, I *promise*. And when it does, you will regret not having these memories with you in them. So just get in there! Do it. Because here's the thing, one or two or twenty years down the road, you will look at that photo of you and your baby when you were both in the thick of it *together* — your hair greasy and shirt covered in spit-up and drool — and you will weep. Tears will flow down your face just as they're streaming down mine right now, and you'll be *so* thankful for that precious moment.

Then as you wipe away the tears, and a smile spreads across your face, you'll realize that there will always be lessons to learn along the way — but there is truly no greater gift than being a mother.

Key Takeaway

Reflect on this author's work and write down one key idea,
concept, or theme that you can take with you in your own life! If
something really hit home, connect with the author and get social!

#5lessons #leadherpublishing

Chapter 3

Ashley Mercer

Author Photo: Julia Francey Photography

Find Ashley: @ash.mercer

From an early age, I was always the babysitter, the mother hen, the caretaker. I had always wanted to be a mom, and while it has come relatively naturally to me, it's not to say there haven't been struggles in my journey through motherhood so far.

Because let's admit it, this mama shit is hard. And while I realize my struggles do not compare to those faced by many marginalized communities, it is my hope that these simple lessons I've learned along the way can help every mama who picks up this book and all of her friends who she passes little bits of info along to.

My name is Ashley Mercer, a mama to one sweet little boy and a newly practicing full spectrum Holistic Doula. For as long as I can re-member, I have loved helping new mothers. Even though I was the oldest cousin, and had always been on babysitting duty, I distinctly remember the first time I really experienced the "fourth trimester."

I was barely fifteen, and an older friend in high school had recently had a baby. I came over to hang out (naively thinking she was going to be ready as soon as I knocked on the door). She needed to shower, she needed to pump, she needed the dishes to be done — and she could not get the baby to sleep. I was able to get the baby to sleep in the time it took her to do the dishes, and she was able to shower. I didn't think much of it until she started to cry. I had NO IDEA then that I would feel so passionately about helping new mothers during pregnancy, postpartum, and the journey that follows.

Five lessons learned, through the journey of motherhood ... that seemed like such a simple topic to write about when I decided to take part in this co-author project. Now that it's time to sit down and write my chapter, I'm riddled with guilt and second-guessing myself. "Who am I to give motherhood advice?"

"I haven't even been a mom for five years ... there has to be a mama out there with more profound advice that should be writing these five lessons."

I have spent years learning about the physical journey to motherhood, how to nurture and support women during that season of their life, and how important that continued support is in the first year and beyond. But actual lessons about being a mom? What the fuck do I, a young mom of one, barely four-year-old, have to contribute?

1. Lose the self-doubt/Mom guilt.

Drop the self-doubt. Seriously, just get rid of it (easier said than done kinda thing, I know!). It's not doing anybody, ANY GOOD. As moms, we are constantly doubting ourselves, comparing ourselves, and overall, thinking we're not doing enough or not doing it well enough. It starts as soon as we find out we're expecting, comparing OB care to Midwifery care and which type of mom uses which. How do you plan to feed your baby? How do you plan to parent? It seemingly never ends. Honestly ... I don't see it getting any easier within the next 18–50+ years either. Overanalyzing and a ridiculous amount of self-judgment seem to come automatically with motherhood.

I'm not quite sure where I first got this strategy, but anytime I'm doubting myself, I ask myself how I would react if my best friend told me she was about to tackle the same task. *Insert writing a chapter on the thing she does 24/7.* I would be ecstatic for her and have no doubt in my mind that she could accomplish it.

If she began to compare herself to the hundreds of thousands of influencer moms on social media, I would berate her with the millions of reasons she is a kick-ass mama, and goddess of a woman Then, I would grant myself the same grace. I'd give myself the same pep talk. We are all doing our very best to navigate this thing called motherhood, and we're all super moms in our own right.

And if you do fail, nobody is actually watching that hard anyway.

2. Mom-cation

So, I probably haven't made this word up, but honestly, the concept is not rocket science: Mom goes on vacation. It doesn't have to be an extravagant island getaway, or an extended trip to the cottage (ALL the power to you if it is, you damn well deserve it, Mama!) As moms, we can all agree how refreshing a few hours alone feels Now imagine every few months or so, you take 24 hours, all to yourself. The kids, home, and pets are all looked after.

Grab a hotel room in town for the night, pack all your favorite self care essentials, a journal, a yoga mat ... whatever you need to enjoy your time to yourself, or with a few girlfriends. Order takeout, dessert AND wine. Have a bath, meditate, catch up on Netflix or Insta gram, go for a hike, or explore a new place.

Whatever it is that you need to recharge your mama batteries, go ahead, and do it. Trust me; leave your mom guilt at home. You deserve this. Your kid(s) and spouse deserve this. Recently, I was feeling drained, absolutely at my wits' end with everything going on and being home with a toddler 24/7. After less than 24 hours of putting myself first, and really spending time with myself, I was able to come home refreshed and grounded. There is nothing I could recommend more to any mom feeling overwhelmed. It is okay to take a step back and put ourselves first.

3. Lonely AF

I'm sure I don't need to tell you that motherhood can be the loneliest you'll ever feel, without ever actually being alone. I find that this isn't something that gets talked about a whole lot, especially for young moms who may be the first among their friend group to have kids. Many friends don't want to intrude on the new parents' first days, weeks, or months, and simply don't know how to be of help. They have no clue how important simple, adult interaction can be to a mom who's been up to her neck in diapers and sippy cups all week.

At least that's how I felt a lot of the time before I was a mom. It wasn't that I wasn't thinking of my dear friends who had just become new parents, it was that I didn't want to be a bother in their already newly chaotic life.

Don't be afraid to ask your friends to show up when you need them. Motherhood can be unnecessarily lonely, and sometimes we do it to ourselves. Don't be afraid to put yourself out there and make new connections. Life happens and friendships fizzle out, but one of the amazing things about motherhood is, there really is a community for everyone.

4. Play

Before we were parents, we were sitting at a playground with some friends and their kids. 'D' looked over at me and kind of stated, "It's always the dads who go and play with the kids, eh? The moms all just kinda come and supervise."

He wasn't wrong, anywhere we went, it always seemed like fun dads, and strict (or boring) moms.

I really didn't give it much thought again, until 'B' was old enough to insist on us playing more imaginative games with him. Often at the most inopportune times ... doing the dishes, cooking meals, folding laundry ... and then one day he said, "Mommy never wants to play with me!"

What 'D' had said that day in the park hit me ... I was the "strict, boring mom." SHIT! How did this happen? We read stories, do puzzles, go on all kinds of adventures ... sure, I'm even the one who orders all the cool toys! But he was right, I wasn't getting on his level, and really PLAYING with him, as often as I should. And why not? There wasn't a single thing on that list that was more rewarding than watching the way his little mind works.

From that day forward, I have made a conscious effort to PLAY more. Really get into his little world and play. And let me tell you, it has made a world of difference. He became more respectful and had way fewer meltdowns almost overnight. And I became much more patient and understanding. The "threenager" stage seemed to melt away when we easily changed our mindset to living more in each moment.

5. You're allowed to do it differently.

While playing with your child may not seem like a groundbreaking revelation, it is something many of us did not experience growing up. We were raised in a generation where parents were very hands-off, and kids were left to mainly entertain themselves. Playing knights and dragons with your littles may be parenting differently than you were parented, and that's okay.

Whether you come from a loving home, with healthy relationships and amazing role models, or you had a traumatic childhood and had to learn things on your own, it's okay to raise your kids differently. It's okay to put in the work for healthier relationships than you had. There is a wonderful mama (hello mastermind behind this project, Courtney!) who said there are no "Permission Police", and I truly believe that goes for parenting as well. I find many of us mamas are so afraid to "mess them up" or "not do it right" that we find ourselves taking advice from those who (no offense) don't have a damn clue what parenting a child in 2020 is like. And, it is completely okay to do things differently, and trust our intuition, as mamas who are raising world-changers. We do not need permission to pave our own journeys through motherhood.

I was afraid my lessons wouldn't be "good enough" but that's the pesky "self-doubt" talking. These are the lessons I have learned. And while they are not learned habits yet, I am making a conscious effort to remind myself of what they have taught me every day. Because of that, I am convinced there are at least a few other mamas out there who could benefit from some of the things that I have learned in my few short years in motherhood.

Key Takeaway

Reflect on this author's work and write down one key idea,

concept, or theme that you can take with you in your own life! If

something really hit home, connect with the author and get social!

....
....
....
....
....
....
....
....
....
....
....
....
....
....
....
....
....
....

#5lessons #leadherpublishing

Chapter 4

Tara Zammit

Author Photo: Savannah Zammit
Find Tara: @tara_zammit

W hen I was younger, I always wanted to be a wife and mom. It was what I knew! It was how I was raised; I feel like it was an expectation and all the women in my life were both. I dreamed about it. I even conjured up names for my future children and wrote them in fancy lettering.

I am one of the oldest grandchildren in my family, and I had lots of younger cousins, so I was always around children younger than me. I even started babysitting when I was 12; I used to babysit my next-door neighbour's children while she was sleeping during the day (she was a nurse and worked through the night). I was never scared because I knew she was home, and my mom was home next door if I needed her.

When I had my daughter, Savannah, I had just turned 22 years old. I felt ready. I felt like, "I can do this!" I've been babysitting and looking after children for the last 10 years … 10 years. I felt comfortable. My husband, Dwayne, didn't necessarily feel the same about his experience, and I have to say, many people doubted I could be a good mom because I was so young.

I am married, and I am the mom of three amazing humans. As I write this, I am 45 years old and have already been a mom for more than half my life! There is a fairly large gap between my children. Their current ages are 23, 19, and 12, and I feel like I am always parenting at three different levels. I have had A LOT of time to learn and apply some of that knowledge. Generally, I have parented my children the same, however, there have been times when I did something differently based on what did (or more so, what didn't) work the previous time.

I worked full-time in the corporate world for the last 24 years, and more recently have been working on building a coaching business that inspires busy moms to reach their health and wellness goals.

1. Sleep? Where are you?

My daughter loved to sleep and I remember thinking how lucky I was and how amazing it was that she slept so well. You'd think I would be sleeping too, but because I was a first-time mom, I kept waking up to see if she was breathing. I would stand over her and put my hand on her chest to make sure it was moving. Back then, video monitors or bed sensors didn't exist! We only had an audio monitor and sometimes it was staticky. Needless to say, I was tired during the day. There were times that I would breastfeed my daughter and fall asleep doing it, or if she took a nap, I would clean the house and do laundry (she spit up on EVERYTHING, including all my tops!).

I thought you were supposed to be 'on' all the time, that you were supposed to be sleep-deprived because it was a mom's rite of passage.

What I didn't think about was, when you first have your baby, you should *absolutely* sleep when your baby sleeps! All the cleaning and everything else you need to do will still be there when you wake up. You will be sleep-deprived, you will be up in the middle of the night, and your baby is going to need you to be ready AND awake.

When my sons were born, they never slept. They would both wake up every 2–3 hours in the night and they NEVER took long naps. They would only sleep if they were feeding or moving. We went on A LOT of walks, which didn't help my sleep situation. It was so much harder to rest because they were number two and three. What did help? The age gap between my kids. When my first son Ryan was born, my daughter was four-and-a-half years old. She went to school for half days and loved to play with her brother when she was home, so I could just lay down beside them while she was playing with him.

When my youngest son, Matthew, was born, Savannah was eleven-and-a-half and Ryan was seven. They were so helpful. They always wanted to watch and play with Matthew and it allowed me to have a little rest.

I learned over the years that sleeping was essential, and it made such a difference in my ability to be a better mom because I was not as sleep-deprived.

2. Ask for help!

Don't feel like you have to do it all on your own. Ask for help from your partner, mom, mother-in-law, friend, sister, or anyone else —especially when it comes to sleep. Ask someone to watch your baby. Don't make the same mistakes I did!

If someone offers their help, take it, and let them know WHAT you need help with. It doesn't help you if they only help with what THEY want to help you with.

It takes a community to raise a child.

I used to hear this when I was young, and I never understood it. I used to feel like I was failing as a mom and wife if I needed to ask for help.

All good moms can do it ALL. Right? NOT! You're still a good mom if you ask for help!

I still struggle with this. I've tried asking for help a few times. People were great. They said "yes" and then they told me what they would do to help. It was rarely what I needed, so I stopped asking.

From a young age, I had my kids start taking on their own tasks, like making their beds. Were they perfect? Absolutely not! Letting go of the need for everything to be perfect allowed me to relinquish control on every single task in our house. I had my children clean up their toys because I learned that if I did it for them, they would make a huge mess. I was enabling them because they knew they could make a big mess and someone else would clean it up. When they learned they had to clean up their own mess, they didn't seem to make such a big one. Who knew?

Asking for help can be in the form of friends and family members when you're sinking in the early stages of motherhood, but don't forget you can start getting your little ones to help you by taking responsibility for small tasks that make a big difference.

3. Trust yourself.

We all navigate our families differently. We raise our children, make decisions, and think, "Am I doing this right?" or "Do I even know what I'm doing?"

Deep down we knew what worked for us. We figured it out; it was a compromise based on his beliefs and mine. It was a challenge at times as we didn't always agree, and we had good days and bad days.

People are generally well-intentioned; they gave advice and told me what they did, and that's really nice of them, but it's what worked for them and their family, so I tried to take it with a grain of salt.

My Mom used to say, "Well that's how I raised you!" Which may have been true and was probably what worked best for her, but times change and that wasn't always what worked for me.

As my children grew, I needed to trust that the values, morals, lessons, and ethics we taught them were being heard (even when I felt like I was talking to a brick wall and they weren't listening to a word I was saying!). I've learned that as they get older and make decisions, our voices play in their heads, and as much as they don't want to hear our voices, they do! As they start their own lives, many of the things that drove me crazy (like clothes all over the floor in their rooms, leaving dishes out, and managing money) will all click. All of a sudden, they won't like that their space is a mess, that the kitchen looks like a disaster when everything is left out, and that their money is more valuable than mine. They may not follow everything that we taught them (they will think, prioritize, and do things differently), however, it will be based on it.

I knew that I knew what was best for my children, even if people gave me unsolicited advice. No one knew my children better than me. I understood the difference in their cries when they were young, and I knew when there was something seriously wrong and they needed medical care. I spent the most time with them, they were talking to me when they cried, and if I listened carefully, they would tell me exactly what they needed. It wasn't easy, but I tried not to let anyone tell me otherwise or let them make me feel like I didn't know what I was doing. Be confident, even if you're a first-time mom.

You've got this! Trust your instincts!

4. Keep showing affection.

I keep kissing and holding my children until they start to pull away. I don't pull away first ... you just never know when they'll be too cool for you. I keep telling them that I love them. I love getting hugs and kisses from them.

Savannah doesn't live at home anymore, so I don't get them as often, but I try to get one when I see her and before we end our visit, I always end our conversations with "I love you."

Ryan will still give me hugs and kisses every morning before he leaves, when he comes home, and before bed.

Matthew loves to cuddle; he will just come up to me out of the blue to give me a kiss or a hug. It's an amazing feeling.

I say, "I love you" a lot to my children. I don't want them to think for a second that I don't, and it's always nice to hear someone say, "I love you." I didn't always hear it growing up, so it's something that I promised myself I would do with my children.

5. Practice self-care.

I wish I knew what self-care was and how important it is when I became a mom. You know, to look after yourself and *then* look after everyone else. It has taken me over 20 years to figure out the importance of self-care. I'm talking specifically about moving my body for at least 30 minutes a day, taking time to be grateful for the little things in life, to meditate, to make intentional eating choices to properly fuel my body, set my daily intentions, and have a positive mindset to make sure I can give my all to my family.

It's not easy to do these things. It takes work! I've been intentionally taking the time in the morning to do most of these things (I do my meditation at night when I'm in bed as it helps me get a better sleep).

I feel like when I got married and became a mom, the expectation and focus was that in order to be good at either or both, I had to put looking after myself aside and give my ALL to my family. It's what I saw, it's what I knew. Exhausted moms trying to do it all and trying to be everything to everyone. Living up to those expectations is IM-POSSIBLE. There is no way to do it without burning out and feeling resentment toward everyone, including those I love most, my husband and my children!

I've lived it, for twenty-three-and-a-half years. I gave everyone my everything; scheduling activities, homework, bedtime, cooking, cleaning, grocery shopping, and anything else that needed to be done. I used to even struggle to get my hair done because I couldn't find the time to go to the salon for 2–3 hours to get it done. I just didn't make *me* a priority.

In 2012, I finally did something for me; I went back to school to get my degree because it was something I knew I needed to do. I did it on top of everything else, including working full time. It took two years, and my family helped where they could, but Matthew was only four years old when I started and he still needed (wanted) me for everything.

My self-care has reduced my stress and reduced the anxiety I was feeling. I have way more energy, my outlook is more positive, and most importantly, I feel like me. I set my intentions and I have my own purpose. Don't get me wrong, I love looking after my family, cooking, grocery shopping, scheduling, etc. But now, I don't feel any resentment because I know I've taken the time to look after myself. After that, giving my all to my family was easy. We all get a piece of the pie, and I think everyone is benefiting from that.

Key Takeaway

Reflect on this author's work and write down one key idea, concept, or theme that you can take with you in your own life! If something really hit home, connect with the author and get social!

Chapter 5
Deanna Collins

Author Photo: K.Thompson Photography
Find Deanna: @deannacollins09

I am beyond excited that I get to share my top five lessons with all of you! My name is Deanna Collins. I have three amazing daughters aged 24, 23, and three, plus a loving and supportive husband. I work for the Ministry of the Attorney General as a Client Service Representative. I've taken a few years off to take care of my youngest and am heading back to work this year. But enough about the present, I want to tell you all how my journey started.

Parenthood began for me when I was 15 years old. When I found out that I was going to be having a baby, I honestly could not have been happier. I remember when my doctor said that I had options and time to think about it, but I immediately said, "I'm keeping the baby." I was super young, but it felt right.

While pregnant, I ended up doing some correspondence courses and attended a school for young pregnant teens. I loved being there with young women going through the same situation as me. Time seemed to fly by and before I knew it, I had a baby girl named Breanna. The struggle was real.

I got little to no sleep and I did not know how to comfort her. Everything was so new and challenging, yet most purely rewarding. From breastfeeding to sore boobs, no sleep, and just trying to take care of myself, I was just trying my best to adapt to the biggest change in my life.

Then, when Breanna was seven months old, I was late for my period. I went to my doctor to do a pregnancy test and found out I was pregnant. When the doctor told me, I started to cry. I was still figuring out how raise a child. I thought, "How am I going to raise another child?" I knew in my heart I needed to keep the baby and in nine months I had another baby girl named Sarah.

I had two little ones to raise and all I kept thinking was that I needed to get an education. So, when Sarah was eight months old, I decided to get my General Education Diploma. I did that plus extra correspondence courses to complete it in less time. I graduated from Grade 12 and then went to college for three years for Legal Administration. Upon graduation, I got accepted fresh out of college to a job with the Ministry of the Attorney General as a Client Service Representative.

After several years, I finally met my husband. We decided we wanted to have a baby! We tried for many years to conceive but unfortunately, had no luck. Finally, at the age of 38, I got pregnant. We were excited but nervous at the same time because I had a miscarriage previously. But we made it, and we had another baby girl named Lila.

I know what you are thinking, "Geez what an age gap," and why after all those years? Well, I genuinely believe that things in our lives are meant to be when they are meant to be. I have learned a lot along the way, and I am still learning. When I think back to when my older daughters were born to now with my three-year-old, it is crazy how many changes have happened, from things to buy or not to buy, sleep coaching, co-sleeping and how to parent your child(ren). Raising two daughters in the '90s to raising one decades later has been different, but also completely similar. The biggest changes have been cell phones and social media.

1. Do not compare yourself to other moms.

This brings me to my first lesson learned through motherhood: Do not compare yourself to other moms. I have had experience with raising children as a young mom and now as an older mom. I have seen how hard it can be for us as moms to compare ourselves to other moms. The looks you get, comments from family, friends and even from people you do not even know.

It is natural as humans to compare ourselves to others, but once you acknowledge it, then move on. As moms, we need to focus on our own strengths, be okay with imperfection, accept where we are on our own journeys, and focus on being grateful for what we have. Remember, we are human, and we are learning. Believe me, no one is perfect!

The biggest change I noticed from raising daughters 20-plus years ago to now, is social media. It can suck you into comparing things at a high level. You follow people that look like they have it all together, but I am sure they do not. You get to see their posts on Instagram, and instantly you are like, "I wish I could look like that; I need to buy that, or she looks perfect." The next time you scroll through social media remember that more than likely they have photoshopped the pictures they are posting to make it look perfect.

2. Be present with your child.

My second lesson learned: be present with your child without distractions such as *cough cough* your cell phone. Having my daughters at different stages of my life, I have learned that children just want your attention and they want to be listened to.

This hit home recently when my third child was two. She kept repeating "Mom" over and over again. I would glance up from my phone and was just not giving her the attention that she needed. This went on for a few days, and I finally noticed that I was sucked into social media. I would just agree to things so I could continue scrolling. A few days went by and then she said, "Mom put your phone down" or "Are you looking at me, Mom?" That's when I knew I had to stop going on my phone when she needed me. I felt completely guilty and sort of sick to my stomach. Suddenly, it clicked, and I told myself, "What are you doing? Your daughter needs you to be present. She will only be this young once." It felt like an addiction. Like I needed to be on it, otherwise, I'd miss out. If you want to mindlessly scroll on social media, maybe try in the morning before the kid(s) are up or after they go to bed. I know we are not perfect, but they are only little once. How do you want to remember your past with your child(ren)?

3. Take the time to do things for you.

The third lesson that I learned is that we all need some form of self-care as moms. If I were to ask myself what self-care was when I was a new mom back in the '90s I honestly would not have known. When I had my older daughters, I went back to school so that I could graduate and then immediately went to college for three years. Once that was completed, I was so excited to get my first job in my field. When I started, I was on contract with no benefits, sick time, or vacation days. I wanted to show my employer that I was serious about my job, and in less than two years, I got hired full-time. I worked my ass off for my children to make a better life for them. Amidst all of this, I was going through a separation with my girls' father (that is another story in itself). I never stopped to take care of myself.

Fast forward to the present, and I now have another daughter who is three years old. I can honestly say that I am just learning what self-care is and what it means to me. To all the moms out there, please take the time to do things for you. It makes you a better mom, wife and friend — and it benefits you more than anything. Self-care can be whatever you want it to be: whether you exercise, read a book journal, meditate, take a walk, or just take a bath.

4. Keep to a routine... as much as possible.

The fourth lesson that I learned is the importance of having a routine. This may or may not resonate with you, but for me it does. Routine has kept me together in many ways. I remember when the two girls were younger, I always had our clothes and lunches ready the night before. I had no time to think when I was getting ready for the day, so it made it easier to have everything ready to just grab and go. This was a big time saver for our busy mornings.

This may surprise you but when the two older girls were small, was not adamant about a strict bedtime routine like I am with my 3-year-old. She has been on a bedtime routine since I stopped breastfeeding her at the age of 15 months. Every child is different but it seemed all I did was breastfeed and I ended up co-sleeping with our youngest daughter. It worked for us for many months and then I felt like we were both ready to change things up. That is when our bedtime routine became extremely important — and it still is. It always starts with a bath after dinner, then brushing teeth, pajama time, and then we read books. We still do this except bath time is not always every night now, and when we sleep elsewhere it can be difficult to stay on routine. Life happens and we adjust but it is key to get back to the routine once you're back home.

5. This too shall pass.

My last lesson learned is: Time will pass. When you become a new mom for the first time, it is hard to even think that you will ever get to sleep again! Tantrums, biting, hitting, growing, and the list goes on and on. I know for me it felt like my children would never sleep and I thought, *How am I going to carry on with my daily needs?* Most days in the very beginning, I lived in my pajamas and rocked the mom bun all the time. Brushing my teeth and showering were hard to come by.

I breastfed all three of my daughters. My third child was the only child I co-slept with; it was the only thing that enabled me to get some sleep. It can be quite upsetting when your baby is in a stage that you are not fond of because I was CONVINCED it would never end. As time passes by, you realize that this too shall pass. No matter what age your child(ren) are, there will always be stages that seem like an eternity, especially when you are in the throes of it all. Trust me, there is an end to stages and they get better as the years go on. Not just in motherhood but in life, things are constantly changing. Just when you think time is standing still, it passes us by. What I recommend taking away from this is to enjoy the precious time we have with our little ones. In the blink of an eye, they are all grown-up and will not need us as much.

Key Takeaway

Reflect on this author's work and write down one key idea,

concept, or theme that you can take with you in your own life! If

something really hit home, connect with the author and get social!

....

....

....

....

....

....

....

....

....

....

....

....

....

....

....

....

....

....

Chapter 6

Chelsea Temple

Author Photo: Adele Sabourin Photography
Find Chelsea: @chelstemple

've always known that I wanted to be a mother. As a child, I would play pretend with my friends and each time I would have between seven and ten kids (which 25 years later, I know is not in my plans — more like two or three). I babysat most weekends and summers and worked as a swimming instructor all through high school and university.

I loved working with kids and I thought motherhood would just come naturally. But, for some reason, when my husband and I decided to start a family, I had so much anxiety that I would be an awful mom or completely mess it up somehow. To add to that anxiety, we had trouble getting pregnant for two years. Needless to say, my anxious mind thought, *Maybe this is a sign that I shouldn't be a mom*. It took me a while, and a bit of therapy, to realize that many people have these thoughts and doubts; that it was normal to be nervous to leap into parenthood. I knew logically that with my experience, personality, and a partner like my husband, we would be great parents!

Being a parent has been the greatest challenge I have taken on, but also the greatest blessing I have ever had! Although I've only been a mother for a year and a half, I have learned some huge lessons and knowledge about myself that I never could have imagined.

1. Strength in numbers... mamas, We need each other!

My son's birth was quite a traumatic experience. After two hours of pushing, I ended up having an emergency C-section and lost a lot of blood. I was in a bit of a fog, not just the "new mom fog", but the low-blood, extreme exhaustion, drugged up on pain meds kind of fog for the first couple of weeks. My anxiety was also making an appearance. I was anxious because I didn't want to be left alone with him. I didn't think I could be a mom by myself. I was also anxious because I didn't feel a huge connection to him; that "bond" they say that you automatically feel as soon as your baby is born. I felt ashamed about it and didn't realize that it was completely normal to feel that way. After talking to some other moms who said the same thing, I felt so relieved.

After a couple of weeks of the two of us on our own, trying to figure each other out, we 'bonded' and I felt that immense mom/baby love. That was when I realized the importance of talking to other moms about every weird, embarrassing, painful, and stressful thing that happens to me. There is guaranteed to be someone in my mom circle who has felt or experienced these things too. Saying my thoughts out loud in my supportive parent-friend group is healthy for me. As parents, we don't need our minds to go down that rabbit hole of shame because parenthood is stressful and busy enough!

2. Every moment is precious!

I know it sounds cliché but seriously, it is! Because I was so "out of it" during my son's first couple weeks of life, when I finally found my bearings, I knew I needed to absorb every single precious moment with this little human. Firstly, because they grow at an exponential speed (or so it seems), and secondly, because I only had 12–18 months with him at 24 hours a day. That time with him was going to expire and decrease to 3–4 hours. I wanted to soak him in. Soak in his sounds, his physical changes, and his milestones as much as humanly possible before I only saw him for a couple of hours a day because, unfortunately, Mama's gotta work.

I am so glad I went into motherhood with this mindset. Don't get me wrong, there have been some sad and frustrating days, but the good have definitely outweighed the bad. When he was around four months old, I loved to sit and watch him discover the new world he was in. I was mesmerized by him. Every day he would learn or do something new. Some days nothing else would get accomplished but that was okay. I'm going to make it my goal to watch him go through life this way. I know I can't be with him 24 hours a day forever, but I'm going to soak in the time I do have with him and not take any of it for granted.

3. My husband isn't a mind reader.

As much as I thought my husband should just know what I wanted or needed when it came to taking care of our baby, he didn't. Like most people, he isn't a mind reader! I finally realized that if I wanted him to do something, I just needed to ask for it. This parenthood thing was new for both of us so it wasn't fair for me to expect that he would just know what he was supposed to do, especially when he went back to work during the first few months after our son was born. Our routine at home and our son's likes and dislikes were changing daily, so on evenings and weekends, I needed to fill him in on what had changed.

This also brings me to the importance of not forgetting about our relationship. It's really easy to fall into only focusing on the baby; creating a routine for the baby, feeding the baby, playing with the baby, researching what I needed to do next for the baby, and so on. This became exhausting and after a few months, I realized that I wasn't thinking about us at all, and that can become very unhealthy. This realization did not come easily and we hit a couple of bumpy days navigating our new life with a baby. We had to learn to not just co-exist but to also thrive together as a family of three and each of us as parents of a new baby. I think we will constantly be learning how to do this.

So, we started planning date nights and we would drop the baby off with our parents. My husband and I even went on vacation for a week and left the baby at home with our parents! Yes, it was extremely hard but we definitely needed it. I'm not saying we have it totally figured out because, heck no, we don't, but we are trying our best to be in a happy and healthy marriage and raise a happy and healthy son.

4. The best plan is no plan.

I wanted to do what would be the least stressful for me and for my baby. When it came to breastfeeding, I said I would try my best but if it didn't work out it was okay. Which ended up being the case. I was too depleted of energy; I wasn't producing much milk at all and he wasn't latching very well. So after about ten days of trying I finally gave it up. I accepted that my mental health (which was struggling) was more important and something had to give, so breastfeeding it was. He had formula from then on with no problems. It relieved a lot of stress.

Also, when it came to sleeping, for the most part, our son was a pretty good sleeper. But we, of course, read all the articles about sleep training and sleep schedules because we wanted him to sleep as much as possible. I tried multiple strategies but I didn't want to get set on one thing in case it didn't work out. You know when you're putting your baby to bed, and you put him in his swaddle sack, give him a soother, rock him while singing 'Twinkle, Twinkle', and lay him in his bassinet with some white noise on, because those things, in that order, worked really well. Then after you lay him down, you go back to bed and close your eyes and start to drift off, and then 'Waaa!' your baby starts crying and wiggles out of his sack and loses his soother. You know that frustrated, end-of-your-rope, almost an-gry feeling you get for a second? Well, I wanted to avoid that. I want-ed to avoid setting myself up for disaster. So, I would do all those things and lay him down and then not lay down myself until he was quiet and asleep for at least a few minutes. Even in the middle of the night, I would scroll Pinterest or Instagram for a while until I knew he was fast asleep. That way I avoided that awful feeling.

So far this 'no plan is the best plan' strategy has worked out for me! I'm also not a Type A person to begin with, so it hasn't been too difficult to do. I want to go into situations with an open mind and be able to adapt if things don't work out how I first perceive they will. I've learned that life throws you curveballs every once in a while, and trying to fight them just makes them last longer and hurt more.

5. Not even a global pandemic can break me!

I mean, it can knock me out for a second, but it can't break me!

We are now in the sixth month of COVID-19 so I have to share my personal experience with it because I have learned so much about myself as a mother. First of all, I learned that my husband and I could be parents all on our own if we absolutely have to. I always thought I wouldn't be able to do it without my "village", although it does make it easier to have access to them. It's nice when our parents take him for the day and I can sleep in, go to yoga, or do things for myself. But, when COVID hit, we had to do everything on our own, with no breaks! And we did it! And it wasn't even that bad! Since we were home so much, we got our baby on a great sleeping routine and all three of us being together 24 hours a day was actually really nice! Our son was learning to walk and my husband didn't miss any of it. We worked together on projects around the house and became stronger as a couple.

The "knock me out" part was how my anxiety surged because of COVID. I am a little bit of a germaphobe already so an invisible sickness that was now a global pandemic threw me for quite the loop! My thoughts spiraled and my anxiety got so bad to the point where I didn't want to leave the house. It was as if I thought the virus was floating in the air and on every surface and I was going to get sick no matter where I went. Thankfully, anxiety was not new for me, and I recognized that my thoughts were irrational and I needed to get on my "recovery train". I made sure that I was taking my medication regularly. I started running most days. I took cold showers when I got home. I did yoga online. And I got in touch with my therapist for a couple "tune up" sessions. My anxiety isn't gone, some days are still hard, but it is much more manageable.

I've finally realized that I need to do regular mental health maintenance, not just wait until my anxiety creeps up. My health — mentally and physically — is more important than ever before, especially since I now have a little human depending on me. I want to be the healthiest version of myself that I can be.

I started listening to podcasts in the car a couple of months into my maternity leave. I felt like I was learning things again and having adult conversations. I felt good about myself; I felt my brain being used for things other than developing a 'sleep, eat, play' schedule (although that is very important). I realized that I needed to keep doing things for myself like listening to podcasts, having discussions with other adults, and opening my mind to worldly topics to expand my brain bubble outside of just motherhood. It is probably the most rewarding and important role I've ever been in, but it's *not all* that I am.

Thinking back to when I was doubting my capability of being a mom, I have to laugh. Our minds can think up some pretty wild scenarios if we let them. I know for a fact that I was born to be a mother. And now, a year-and-a-half into parenthood, I feel like I am thriving. I'm sure I won't always feel this way, but I'm going to do my best to take the wins when I can get them and learn from any mistakes that I make.

Key Takeaway

Reflect on this author's work and write down one key idea, concept, or theme that you can take with you in your own life! If something really hit home, connect with the author and get social!

Chapter 7
Terri-Ann Perras

Author Photo: Amanda Greer Photography
Find Terri-Ann: @terriannmichelle

"Pet Peeve: Children."
Based on my life today, you probably wouldn't believe that this was part of my Grade 6 yearbook statement — and to be honest, it was my motto for the better part of my life. I could never understand why anyone would want to give up their free time, time with their partner, date nights, club nights, vacations and ultimately their body — to spend the rest of their life taking care of another human.

I thought maybe when I met the "right" one, I would change my mind. I figured I'd fall in love and immediately want to procreate because that's what the fairy tales always told us. I was wrong, again. After marriage (to the most incredible husband), I was so far invested in my personal growth, my health, and fitness (I was competing nationally at fitness shows) that giving up my body was even more terrifying than ever. I had worked so hard to be where I was, why would I want to give all that up? I wasn't ready to be selfless and I definitely wasn't ready for motherhood.

I'm not sure what changed me. It seemed like I just woke up one day and my whole world felt different. I can't say I felt "ready," because to be honest, two kids later (and one on the way), I'm still not "ready" — but I just felt like it was time. It was time to find out what everyone was talking about when they said, "You don't know what love is until you have a child," and boy were they right.

Motherhood didn't come easy for me. I didn't just fall into it as the age-old tale often describes. I always thought it would be instinctual; that I'd just miraculously know what to do. I remember coming home after my first son was born, sitting on the couch and staring at him in amazement that I had created this tiny human, so sweet and perfect — and then it hit me. I immediately felt unworthy, unqualified, terrified and so uncertain. I recall looking at my husband and saying, *"What now?"* What was I supposed to do if he cried? What if his diaper is dry, and he's fed, but he just won't sleep? Do I rock him? Feed him more? Is there something wrong? Am I doing something wrong? No matter how many baby books you read (...I assume, anyway, since I didn't read any — and I don't regret it) or how many classes you take — nothing prepares you for *actual* motherhood. Motherhood is something that comes with time, patience, and perseverance. You're going to make mistakes (a lot of them!), and you'll have good days and bad days. Some days feel like they go on forever like you can't do anything right — and some days will feel like one giant victory. It's a damn roller-coaster — but the best and most rewarding adventure you'll partake in.

Over the past five years, I've learned a lot about myself. I've suffered deeply — emotionally and physically — and I lost myself somewhere along the way. I've overcome postpartum depression (PPD) (*twice*) — and with that, a lot of my personal relationships suffered as did my relationship with myself for a long time. With a lot of counselling, soul searching, learning to let go, and adjusting to this new normal, I've learned a lot of lessons along the way. I'm Terri-Ann and these are five of the most important lessons I've learned from my journey through motherhood (so far).

1. You'll never love two kids the same.

I love my first child so much. How will I ever have another, and love them *this* much? I asked myself this question for a *long* time before we decided to have baby number two. It weighed on me so heavily that I almost didn't have another. Even while I was pregnant, I spent the entire time convinced that there was NO way I'd ever love a baby as much as I did my firstborn. It ate me alive. I felt like my second born was just going to get whatever love I had leftover — and it wouldn't be fair. It wouldn't be enough. But here's the truth — you WON'T. You will never, EVER, ever, ever (I would keep going, but I have a word limit here!) love another child "as much as" you do your firstborn. You will love them fully and completely to your core, but in unexplainably different ways. Each in their own way, for different reasons. They will own a whole new section of your heart that you never knew existed. You will never love them the same way you did your first. You will simply love them differently. And it's magical.

2. What works for one, will not always work for the other.

It's time to learn to adapt! This is something that people tell us often when we're about to have baby number two — and quite frankly, I find it annoying. "You don't get lucky twice," or "Your second born won't sleep as well as your first," *Blah blah blah*. It used to make me furious. And then I lived it — and man is it true. No two babies are the same. Period. Every technique I learned to soothe, put to sleep, feed, change, bathe, rock, hold, or swaddle my first child did NOT work the second time around.

I felt like I was a first-time mother all over again. It was frustrating. I thought I had it all figured out — and then all of the sudden I had no idea what I was doing. *But that's exactly what motherhood is all about.* Here is my advice: take off those pants full of expectation, remove that badge of honour you got for finally figuring out this whole parenting thing — and get ready to go back to parenting school. (Don't worry, you'll win the war again one day!)

3. Let go of who you were and embrace who you're about To become.

This is something I struggled with for a VERY long time. My postpartum journey after my firstborn was rough, to say the least. I suffered from PPD, severe anxiety, and I shut myself off from the world. I spent every ounce of energy I had taking care of my child, and very seldom myself, and then I didn't have time for anyone else.

When I came out on the other side, I struggled with the loss of friendships, my lack of interest in the partying scene, and ultimately, my complete change of personality. My struggle surrounded the ongoing pressure to "not forget who you used to be", but the fact was, I *wasn't* the same person. I loved who I had become. I felt things deeper, saw things more clearly, cared more about the little things, and a lot less about shit that didn't matter. When I finally let go of who I used to be and embraced who I had become, life became a lot more beautiful and a lot less lonely. Which brings me to my next point ...

4. Motherhood is LONELY.

Even though I don't get a second to myself (like, ever) — it's still the loneliest place I've ever been. HOW is it lonely then? (I can hear you yelling at me!) Here's why: the loneliness was in my head. It took me a long time to realize that. For whatever reason, I always felt like every battle I was facing, I was doing it alone. I felt guilty asking for help (I'm a mom, I should be able to just do this on my own, right?) I never wanted to talk about things. I internalized my resentment, my sadness, my exhaustion, and I suffered for a long time — Until the day I asked for help. That's when I realized that the tale is true — it takes a village to raise a child. So, here's my advice: let go of your expectations of YOURSELF. Remember, it's okay to ask for help. Emotional, physical, psychological, spiritual — any form of help you feel you need. Just ask. The moment I accepted that this journey couldn't be traveled alone — was the moment my life changed for the best.

5. Live one day at a time.

Motherhood is full of obstacles, emotions, learning, mistakes, victories, hard times, and the best times of your life. It's a journey that without a doubt needs to be taken one day at a time. The following poem has been near and dear to my heart since as far back as I can remember for reasons unrelated to motherhood. But through my hardships and experiencing mom guilt, it brought new meaning to every word. So, I will leave you with this, and I hope that on your hard days you can find comfort in these words too.

Two Days We Should Not Worry

There are two days in every week about which we should not worry,
two days which should be kept free from fear and apprehension.

One of these days is Yesterday with all its mistakes and cares,
its faults and blunders, its aches and pains.

Yesterday has passed forever beyond our control.
All the money in the world cannot bring back Yesterday.

We cannot undo a single act we performed;
we cannot erase a single word we said.
Yesterday is gone forever.

The other day we should not worry about is Tomorrow
with all its possible adversities, its burdens,
its large promise and its poor performance;
Tomorrow is also beyond our immediate control.

Tomorrow's sun will rise,
either in splendour or behind a mask of clouds, but it will rise.
Until it does, we have no stake in Tomorrow,
for it is yet to be born.

This leaves only one day, Today.
Any person can fight the battle of just one day.
It is when you and I add the burdens of those two awful eternities
Yesterday and Tomorrow that we break down.
It is not the experience of Today that drives a person mad,
it is the remorse or bitterness of something which happened Yesterday
and the dread of what Tomorrow may bring.
Let us, therefore, Live but one day at a time.

— Author Unknown

Key Takeaway

Reflect on this author's work and write down one key idea, concept, or theme that you can take with you in your own life! If something really hit home, connect with the author and get social!

Chapter 8

Amy Bridle

Find Amy: @amybridle

Can I tell you a secret? Something that single-handedly, subtly, and pervasively derailed my life and impacted the possibility of me ever becoming a mama? It's embarrassing to admit, but before meeting my wonderful husband in 2009, and starting our family in 2013, I spent a total of almost 13 years in two separate, but back-to-back relationships that were abusive to some degree. Fool me once, shame on you. Fool me twice, shame on me . . . right?

Wrong. I had always dreamed of getting married and having children. That was not something I ever thought wouldn't happen for me. I just kept thinking it would "get better" or they would "change their minds." Never did I think, "Well shit, I guess I should look elsewhere to find a man whose values and dreams align with my own!"

So there I was after 13 years of being gaslit, manipulated, emotionally terrorized, financially drained, occasionally choked, and physiologically blackmailed ... 32, single, and living back home in my small Ontario town with my parents! EPIC LIFE FAIL! Or so I thought. Back then, I had no idea what "gaslighting" was. No idea what "cognitive dissonance" was. No idea what "narcissistic personality disorder" was. I still struggle to comprehend all of it.

What I was, was kind, compassionate, empathetic, and optimistic of other peoples' potential despite their actions. Perhaps I was naive, but I was blessed to be raised to see and hold on to the best in people. This ended up being my greatest strength along with my greatest weakness. Despite the trauma I experienced, I still upheld those values and lived from a place of possibility. I also acknowledge that this makes me very privileged. I am forever grateful for my parents' support both financially and emotionally, and the support of my wonderful community.

I wasn't educated in setting boundaries, human behaviour, attachment theory... seriously who is? I was a young woman desperate to love and be loved in return. I wanted so badly to have babies. To create a family. But it could have *not* happened. I could have been duped into a childless existence. Or worse, I could have had babies with one of those two men — and good lord, that would have been awful!

But this chapter isn't about my past, it's an introduction to who I am. Today and every day, I choose love. If you recognize any of the signs in the words I've written above let me yell it from the rafters: YOU ARE NOT CRAZY! YOU ARE NOT ALONE! YOU CAN RECOVER! YOU DESERVE ALL OF YOUR DREAMS ... AND ALL OF YOUR BABIES!

It is time that concepts, like those I've mentioned, become common knowledge to girls and women. It's time that we educate our partners and sons. And while this isn't a book about abuse, my experiences have made me who I am and have influenced how I parent.

My name is Amy. I am an actor, author, entrepreneur, theatre arts educator, podcast co-host, and self-care guru ... and these are the five things that I've learned through motherhood.

1. I am such an A-HOLE!

There I was, two days postpartum after the birth of my first child, rocking back and forth in the nursery rocker and just staring in awe at the sleeping baby in my arms. Rocking. Rocking. Rocking. It's a hormonal time ladies, I get that. I found it hard to not have her physically in my arms *at all times!* I literally ached if someone took her so I could sleep, or eat, or recover, or shower. I felt manic and woke up searching the house to snatch my baby away from whoever was tending to her or watching her sleep. P.S. Newborns babies sleep a lot so I probably could have chilled the 'F' out!

I felt a bit out of control and crazy. I was confused by this new intensity — a maternal magnetism. So, as I said, there I was, sitting in that rocker methodically rocking the fuck out of it when it suddenly hit me. And when I say, "hit me," I mean that it literally felt like I had been simultaneously gut and throat punched by Mike Tyson the heavyweight champ. I gasped for air. Tears like I have never experienced flooded forth. The constriction in my throat and chest was as though I was being crushed by the world's largest boa constrictor. And one singular thought formed with crystal clarity in my consciousness ... "Oh my God! This is how much my mother loves me? I am such an ASSHOLE!"

All the times I sassed her. All the times I thought I knew better and treated her like garbage. All the times I lied. All the times I was disrespectful, didn't listen, or didn't call. The sheer magnitude of her love and my ignorance brought me to my knees and for the first time in my life I truly understood how gorgeously painful it was going to be for me to be a mother. So that's the first lesson, ladies. Being a mama is going to hurt like sweet hell. They will test you, sass you, disrespect you, ignore you, lie to you, and forget to call. But one day they may hold their own baby and suddenly realize why you are "crazy." Crazy in love.

2. Remember! You are the architect of your dreams.

Remember that secret that I told you in my intro? The one about being 32, single, and living at home? There I was, trying to make sense of my life, trying to heal, and desperately trying not to let the fear of not having babies control me. I casually mentioned to my mom, "No Bigs! If I haven't found someone to build a family with by the time I'm 35, I'm going to just have a baby on my own." Her response was NOT what I was expecting. It was very triggering for her. At that time, she had her ideas and opinions about what a "family" should look like and what I was describing, was not it! In effect, I got "should on."

This lesson is a short one and honestly applies to all things in life. I lucked out and met a wonderful partner to create a family with. However, I want you to know that whoever you are, wherever you are, and for whatever reason, you are the architect of your dreams. If motherhood is something you aspire to, then never let anyone "should on" you. Whatever your age, sex, gender, relationship status, race, religion, ability, etc., I am hereby giving you permission to have children — whether you birth them, adopt them, foster them, surrogate them, or manifest them. I'm not promising it will be easy, but the decision is yours and yours alone.

3. There's always a reason and you know what it is.

"A Mother's Intuition"... ever heard of it? Probably. I think it's ingrained in our culture. The shit end of the stick, however, is that modern mamas are so inundated with images and opinions from Facebook and

Instagram that we've forgotten how to listen to our inner voice — our guts. After seven years, and two beautiful kiddos, I can honestly say this ... I have tortured myself trying to get it right. I have let others' opinions influence my feelings, I've let what I think is "supposed" to be right guide my decisions. But after all is said and done, I can tell you this: every time I have ignored my gut feelings, every time I have not followed my intuition, every time I have not honoured what I know deep down is best for MY children, I have paid the price. Listen to your beautiful and unique inner voice. Let your feelings guide you. You are the one who knows your child the best. You have been blessed with that job; *you* are the expert. Honour yourself, and in doing so you will always honour your babes and make the best, right choice, at that moment!

4. You're no good to anyone when you are all 'give.'

Straight up! At six months postpartum with my second child, after not sleeping for two-and-a-half years and going through a second pregnancy at a very high weight, I had a full-on health disintegration.

I won't bore you with the details but the reality is if I had embraced or even vaguely understood the concept of self-care before having children, then I can guarantee I could have avoided a lot of sickness and stress. The thought of not being there to watch my babies grow, of not being a vibrant and healthy woman, of not living my best life — was crippling. I had to wake up and really understand that I could only truly take care of my family when I took care of myself!

Self-care at its heart is a return to yourself. It's a path towards self love. This experience ignited a passion and resolve in me to not only develop a self-care practice myself, but to create a community of women who wanted to do the same. A community that understands that our needs in relation to ourselves may differ, but that one thing remains the same ... we are in this together, sisters.

5. "The days are long, but the years are short."

God love me, the poem "On Children," by Khalil Gibran. But even before I had ever laid eyes on this beautiful piece of writing, I had always felt this quote in my bones... my exhausted, unbalanced, newly mom'ed bones. You see, one of my closest friends was killed in a freak car accident when we were ten. I lost three babies to miscarriage before I finally had my daughter. One of my closest friends from high school experienced a dramatic and devastating stillbirth. A close acquaintance of mine lost two full-term babies back-to-back.

I knew intellectually and statistically that lots of people had beautiful healthy babies, but I was so jaded and full of anxiety about the preciousness and blessing that is new life. Everywhere I looked, I just seemed to see or experience pain, and loss, and grief, and fucking unfairness. I was so fully aware of how fragile the entire process could be. So when the beautiful Miss B fell into my arms and then couldn't feed properly for the first three months of her life; or couldn't sleep for more than 45 minutes at a time; who didn't sleep through the night till she was almost four (and who still struggles at seven); who I witnessed struggle neurologically with sensory processing challenges; I never had to look far to remember, reframe, and honour all those who have lost.

I would be delirious with sleep deprivation, but I would always be able to reach for gratitude. I would be crazy with worry about her development, but I would always be able to breathe and remind myself that I was the luckiest mama in the world at that moment. She was happy, she was healthy, she was mine ... and that was all I ever needed.

It is true, mamas, when you have your babies, time switches simultaneously into cartoon slow-motion and time-lapse fast forward. Imagine that sensation. It feels like something is ripping inside your body. You are chronically torn between exhaustion and awe, bullshit and beauty. Your brain just cannot maintain balance. But I urge you and remind yourself: YOU ARE THE LUCKIEST. And when you're in the days that feel so long, just breathe, take some space, and remember you are blessed. Like really fucking blessed! So many would give anything to have just one more minute with the babies and children they've lost. I remember those angels and I honour them and their mamas' pain.

Motherhood has taught me that reframing any hard situation can help, because believe me, I'm seven years in, and I honestly have no idea where the time went or how they got so big. Like I said, it's beautiful bullshit! So, count the small moments, put down your phone, remind yourself that hard seasons pass, and that truly — before you can comprehend it — these precious years will be a thing of the past. But have no fear, if you're really lucky, they will move back in with you when they're 32.

Key Takeaway

Reflect on this author's work and write down one key idea, concept, or theme that you can take with you in your own life! If something really hit home, connect with the author and get social!

....
....
....
....
....
....
....
....
....
....
....
....
....
....
....
....
....
....

#5lessons #leadherpublishing

Chapter 9
Jennifer Sawyer

Author Photo: Adriana Wilkin Photography
Find Jennifer: @northend_fitness

Hi, my name is Jen. Well, my friends call me Jen. As do most people who meet me for the first time. To my family, my name is Jennie. At school, I'm Mrs. Sawyer and when I teach fitness classes at North End, I am Jennifer. Friends from high school still call me Orav, a play on my maiden name. I guess that's what happens when you're an early '80s baby born with the most popular name of the year. You have to get creative to stand out and not just be "Jenny O" for the rest of your life. Which name do I go by the most? None of these, actually. Instead, it's "Mommy!" Sorry, it's more like "MMMOOOMMMMMMEEEEE!" and is usually paired with a time sensitive need of sorts. *sigh* Let's start again.

Hi, my name is Jennifer. I go by Jen or Jennie (or Mrs. Sawyer) but my favourite people call me Mom. I love to teach. I love to share. I love to empower women and I am inspired by those who strive to do the same. Therefore, when I discovered this project, I saw a chance to teach, to share, and to empower a fellow MMMOOOM-MMMMMEEEEEEE (sorry, it's annoying right?) on the journey of motherhood. I thought it may be helpful that I pass on a few of the lessons I have learned in my ten years of being a mom so far. I do so with a strong and genuine hope that someone may relate to a piece of the anxiety or a pinch of the panic that I have experienced. Plus, I wanted to show Clara, Grace, and Haydyn that they can achieve anything they desire and I have always wanted to write for an audience. Manifestation complete. So, girls, this one's for you. And for me. And for the mom feeling overwhelmed at Walmart. I promise, you'll be okay.

***

Before becoming a "Mommy" to not one, not two, but three beautiful girls, I would have told you that I, more or less, thought I had life figured out. I felt in control of my feelings, knew my goals for the future, and was immensely prepared throughout my daily routine. I had just the right amount of change in my car for my morning Tim's, and consistency was key. I prioritized my physical health either by attending or instructing fitness classes daily and made a cognizant effort to take care of my mental well-being. Before you throw this book across the room, I admit that I'm making it sound like life was all sunshine and rainbows. Of course, it was not, but in retrospect, it was simple, and I felt in charge. A healthy, happy balance between alone time, girls' nights out, family visits, and date nights with my husband, Jamie. All in all, life just worked. It flowed like these ideas are now, and I was doing what I loved while feeling in control. So, what happened?

Well, when I found out, with joy, that I was pregnant with our oldest daughter, Clara, I assumed life would continue on this carefree path, but with a baby beside us. You schedule the baby to meet your lifestyle, not the other way around, right? Not the case. On an early Tuesday morning, I was awoken off guard by a sudden and significant gush that pulled my eyes wide open. I rolled over to discover meconium from a baby girl who decided that she wanted to come almost three weeks early — to a mom who was not prepared. In a panic, I absorbed the idea that my hospital bag was not yet packed and pondered the — I now admit, useless — list of things that I still had to do: clean the bathroom, wash my hair, cook and freeze another dinner for two. *"How could it be time?" "But I'm not ready!"* These scattered thoughts spun as we got in the car and drove to the New Life Centre where our baby would be born. Adrenaline was shooting through my body alongside the recognition that this was not how the planner in me wanted things to go. But WANT, it turns out, is often the antonym to IS when you are a mom. An important lesson was quickly becoming apparent:

1. Motherhood is not something that you will ever be fully prepared for.

As I embraced this new role, my Type A personality was challenged and I was learning how to bend, or at least become a little more flexible. And so, from what I now recognize to be a minor change of plans, I learned a teeny lesson on letting go of expectations, plans and norms. I learned that it is all right (it really is!) to not be fully prepared for everything and that it is okay to not be in control. Let me say it again to convince myself as I type it: it is OKAY to NOT be in control. But let's be real. My water breaking and our baby arriving sooner than her due date was certainly not even close to enough to disrupt my life. However, experiencing multiple panic attacks and developing severe postpartum anxiety after weaning that nursing baby sure was. The first panic attack that I can clearly recall and labe was in the diaper aisle in Walmart with Clara in the shopping cart. One second, I was reading the ingredient list on a lanolin product, and the next thing I knew, I was overcome with an intense and disturbing fear. This senseless feeling appeared suddenly like a spiteful raincloud opening up and violently unloading its contents onto unaware me. I felt incredibly sick to my stomach, immensely dizzy, and was certain I was going to pass out. My pulse was racing uncontrollably and I was drenched in sweat, numbed with terror. I didn't know whether to scream for help or run out of the store. I leaned on the cart, head down, and eventually breathed myself out of the episode. I felt green. I quickly paid for the items I had found and sped to my car where I texted Jamie about what had happened. Nothing made sense. Together, we summed it up to me being either hungry or dehydrated and needing to rest. After all, no one sleeps or eats properly with a new baby in their lives. Unfortunately, it was more than just sleep-deprivation or thirst that brought on that and countless other attacks of its kind.

One of the very upsetting episodes that I experienced happened with co-workers over a dinner meeting. When our food arrived, I was unable to eat. I used a fork to place salad in my mouth but physically could not swallow the lettuce. A steel trap door was closed tight at the top of my throat and I was once again overcome with fear, panic, and dizziness. I felt clammy and warm; I was out of control. When I had to leave the group early by faking an oncoming stomach flu, I got in my car and bawled. What was happening to me? I had no schema to understand what was going on. I just knew that a force stronger than myself was taking over my brain and body and was disrupting my world — I was struggling to eat, to sleep, to live. I was failing to breathe without fear. I knew this was not sustainable and that I could not be a mom if I could not even be myself. Eventually, these attacks led to a debilitating fear of leaving the house and of being around crowds. I misplaced control over my thoughts, losing the ability to differentiate between real and worry. My confidence in my ability to easily do things that I once took for granted: going

to restaurants with friends, church with family, the gym by myself...
disappeared, and what was left of life with a baby was upside down.
After many brutal months of suffering from "the monster" I call anxiety, I learned from my GP that it's common and acceptable for new
moms to experience this and I learned that...

2. ... One of the best things I could do was to reach out for help.

When I met the psychologist, who diagnosed me with postpartum anxiety and validated everything I was feeling, I knew I would
overcome this obstacle. Using Cognitive Behavioural Therapy (CBT),
I was able to alter my current state and regain control of my mental
well-being. I went into my second pregnancy with our middle girl,
Grace, with a new insight into what it meant to have it together and
to be prepared. I weaned her slowly to avoid the hormonal crash that
we now suspect led to the initial feelings of anxiety with Clara. Another lesson was learned:

3. When we alleviate fears from the past and press forward, we can use our nightmares to create our dreams.

With two babies under the age of two, I learned to let go more.
When our clumsy preschooler was concussed from walking into a
parked car (you can't make this stuff up), I used my novel flexibility

to care for her and handle the situation without worry. I preferred this composed self over the turbulence I had experienced as a mom thus far, and I was motivated to apply this calm to all areas of life moving forward. Therefore, when we ecstatically discovered that we were pregnant with our third baby, I was determined to remain peaceful and carefree during her delivery. With certainty, I knew I would adapt and manage, labouring at home until it was just the right time to arrive at the hospital.

Haydyn was born in a parking lot. The hospital parking lot. The experience was crazy. Intense. It was scary and cold. Freezing, icy, silver, and bright blue-grey cold. To be factual, it was during a polar vortex in February in Ontario, Canada and I was without clothes from the waist down. Cold. But it was fine. And so was I. A doula and Jamie delivered our baby girl with a nurse who sprinted outside just in time to witness my baby's bottom half appear. Without hesitation and at a rapid pace, Haydyn was rushed inside to the warm hospital, a happy, healthy girl. After taking those extraordinary and unsteady strides on my path through motherhood, I was convinced that I had mastered how to accept life as it comes. Here I was, back in control. I had planned for Haydyn's birth to go a certain way and when it didn't, I accepted it. I knew then that the next time I ended up in an unsolicited situation, I would approach the whole event with an open mind. Motherhood continued to prepare me for the unimaginable. And then a global pandemic hit.

I got sick. Really sick. Doctors suspected I had COVID-19 and kept testing me for the disease. For five days, I was isolated in a hospital room where I did not eat, drink, or sleep, and worst of all, my children were not allowed to come and see me. This ignited the return of anxiety and panic attacks, which flooded back like a tsunami, destroying rows of homes and every pillar of stability I had created. The monster was back and I had no control. I was no longer able to just let things happen or to utilize any of the skills that motherhood had taught me. I lost the ability to handle what came my way. More than anything, I missed my kids. After days of tests and tears, it was confirmed that I had appendicitis but was unable to receive an operation. I spent three weeks in and out of hospitals where I was struck with guilt about not being able to mother my girls. I wanted nothing more than to be a mom at home, stressing about my kids constantly calling me, "MMMOOOMMMMMMEEEEEEE," and pressing me with all sorts of nonsensical requests. When I had no choice but to stay in the hospital, I had to let go of how I would have done things at home and be content that Jamie was able to care for our daughters. Once again, motherhood was challenging me to "let it be." As expected, I ended up in emergency surgery and was soon sent home where my sweet family took care of my recovery. Our youngest kept directing me to "just breathe in; breathe out." Her simple insight on how to handle stressful situations was something I had shared with her before, and it reminded me that my girls digest every word that I speak. I knew that Haydyn was right, in this circumstance, and in general.

4. Being a mom is often about just breathing in and breathing out. Embrace life as it comes.

One deep inhale and long release at a time. Through motherhood, I have learned that I can change and that I can let go. I can be a panicked new mom in Walmart or a shocked woman delivering a newborn in a blustery parking lot. I can be surprised by a baby with meconium or a scared mom needing surgery and separated from her children. Through it all, I have learned that I will always be perfect. Perfectly unprepared, that is. And that I will be okay. It is now that I see, with clarity, that motherhood has gifted me many lessons I have learned to be prepared for the unprepared, to reach out for help when needed. I have learned to use past nightmares to guide future situations and to embrace life as it comes. I recognize now that the fifth lesson is simple:

5. Remember the importance of sharing your story with other moms.

I want to share my discovery that motherhood is an unpredictable road of highs and lows, of dark and light, and one that you will never truly feel ready for. You will be in and out of control. You will have plans that run smoothly and expectations that fall apart. You will feel happy, then sad, scared, then secure. This is all part of your story. To the mom who feels unprepared, scared, panicked, or overwhelmed, my advice is to slowly let go, ride the wave, and reach out to someone for help. Remember that motherhood will make you strong and resilient and that MMMOOOMMMMMMEEEEEEE (sorry!) will be okay.

Key Takeaway

Reflect on this author's work and write down one key idea,

concept, or theme that you can take with you in your own life! If

something really hit home, connect with the author and get social!

....
....
....
....
....
....
....
....
....
....
....
....
....
....
....
....
....
....
....
....

#5lessons #leadherpublishing

Chapter 10
Amanda Sarria

Author Photo: Andrea Trifunovic, Blue Orchid Creations
Find Amanda: @amandasarria

"Mrs. S., will your husband be joining us?" the ultrasound technician asked as she squirted the jelly onto my 9-week pregnant, overfilled bladder causing me to catch my breath as I practiced my very first Kegel (moms y'all know what I am talking about). I let her know that he was running late but would be here.

"Oh good!" she exclaimed, "because there are two heartbeats in here, I'd love for him to see."

My body jolted up so quickly, causing the probe to drop and the table to shake: "TWO?" I asked in a panicked, unsure, kind of excited voice. "Two, Mrs. S.," and she held up two fingers with one hand as she guided me back down to a lying position on the table.

I could feel my eyes begin to well up just as there was a knock at the door and in walked my smiling husband. "Sorry I'm late," he began.

"TWO!" I blurted out, holding up two fingers with one hand and my belly with the other. I could see the same amount of panic, unsureness and excitement cross his face, just as I was feeling, but then he sat down beside me, reached for my hand, and said, "That's great, let me see my babies."

At that moment, my panic left and excitement set in as we started our journey as twin parents. Surely, we could do this, right? We weren't the first people having twins, and we certainly wouldn't be the last. Millions of questions began to unravel in my head as the technician asked, "Are there any questions before we wrap up?"

I had a ton to ask but was going to just politely say "No thank you" and spend the next few days googling, but instead, I blurted out, "Please just check and confirm that there isn't a third heartbeat."

Just 37.6 weeks later (I've skipped over the nine months of throwing up all day, every day, while teaching kindergarten, because well, it definitely wasn't a highlight), we were ready to take home our twins. Except that we pulled into our driveway and stopped and stared at each other... both thinking (and shortly after saying), what, the actual, fuck ... what were we supposed to do? Where did all the parenting course lessons we took go? Did we miss the information from the hospital on what to do when we brought the babies home? We had absolutely no clue on what to do — but quickly, together with our village — we figured it out.

Motherhood is one of the scariest, fulfilling, exciting, frightening journeys to be on, and while I've only been leading my tribe for six short years (depending on the day of the week you ask me), the amount of learning I have done has been monumental.

I am Amanda, wife to Carlo, Mama to twins Noah and Charlotte, daughter, sister, aunt, cousin, godmother, friend, educator, lover of coffee, wine, and solo grocery trips, and this is what I have learned on my ever-evolving journey through motherhood.

1. Advice—Accept it and file it.

Motherhood is arguably the most difficult and influential job on the planet, yet there are no rules or guidelines outlining how to actually do it. So, what do we do? What do we do when we have this precious baby (or in my case, two) that we are responsible for?

We do what every mother did before us and what every mother will do after us — we figure it out.

Natural birth or medicated? Vaccines? Breastfeeding or formula? Organic? There are a plethora of opinions, countless books to read, a ton of friends, cousins, random ladies at the grocery stores who have experience — but it's just that — their OWN damn experience, not yours. Do not allow someone else (even if you respect them and they mean well) to determine how you will parent.

Do I vaguely remember the first time I was offered unsolicited advice? Yes. Was I devastated that I was being judged by a little smiling 80-something-year-old? Yes. But at that moment, I did what I did, because I needed to, and I shouldn't have to explain my decisions or choices to anyone, even the sweet old lady who meant well. Things happen and lessons are learned. That's right, a lesson — not a mistake — because you learn and evolve from each experience you have.

You are going to mess up a whole lot, Mama, but guess what? That is okay. It is part of this whole parenting gig we signed up for. Parenting is hard. It is extra hard when you are given unsolicited advice, and it is okay to shut it down before it is given. Trust yourself. Do what is best for you, your family, and most importantly that little babe in your bed (or crib if that's how you chose to parent). Advice is just that, an opinion. And in the wise words of my sister cousin, "Appreciate the advice and use it when you see fit — in other words, file it with a smile and move on."

2. The little things actually do matter.

Lessons are guiding principles that help us to navigate the world a little easier. Nothing is written in stone. However, if there is anything I have learned in my short time of being a mama, it is that the little things you do matter to your kids. It's not the revolutionary things that we try to achieve that matter, just the everyday ordinary acts.

Insert proud Mama moment — my husband and I take pride in the compliments we receive on how well our children treat others — why and how, you might ask? Because it's equally important to us that we make every person we come into contact with feel appreciated. We say, "Good morning!" and "How are you?" to neighbours, strangers, etc. We show that gratitude goes a long way, especially with our favourite Tim Hortons manager (who we see more frequently than we should) or like our friendly neighbour (aka Neighbourhood Watch) whose driveway we shovel at every snowfall and hair we cut hair every few weeks. We take time out of our day to treat others how we hope to be treated. Our kids have not only picked up on it, but have integrated these behaviours into their daily interactions.

We are transparent (at an age-appropriate level) about what is going on in the world. Our children have learned about the hardships marginalized groups face just for being who they are, and we have taught them to stand up for those who might be voiceless. We march, we protest, we raise money, we rally behind those who need it — it's just what our family does.

You see, it isn't about the failures, it's about how we get back up and recover that is most important. We have suffered loss and fear and failure, but we do it together and we share our vulnerabilities, and by our example, our children have become empathetic, caring, thoughtful human beings who we are damn proud of.

3. You were someone before you were a mama.

If there is any piece of advice that you take away from me, please make it this: DO NOT forget about you. It took me six whole years to find myself again, and wow, does it feel good to be me (a different me, but a me I am totally digging these days and my husband is too, if y'all feel me).

I can only write from experience, but in speaking with my #twin-mamaclub (you ladies know who you are) this idea of remembering who we were before we were Mama is especially hard for us. When you have two newborn babies you kind of do this divide and conquer thing, which from a relationship standpoint works well, but it also means there is no real time for you.

Do not forget about you. I'm not talking about taking a #self-caredayselfie on Instagram while at the spa all day. (If you can do that, amazing, if you can't, don't dismiss what self-care might look like for you.) I'm talking about taking the time to appreciate yourself and those beautiful babies you made. You are important and worthy of care and love, so take those extra five minutes in the washroom scrolling Instagram, or sit for a few extra minutes in the driveway while the babies nap and enjoy that hot coffee, or perhaps your win is a midday shower at nap time, or enjoying a yoga/run session. Whether it's a grocery run with your besties, a bitch session with the ladies, or a drink during happy hour — take it! It's the small wins that truly do help in recognizing your worth, replenishing your metaphorical cup, and ensuring that you don't forget who you were before you were Mama. Taking care of you is not optional; it's necessary for survival.

4. Keeping score never ends well!

Stop counting the things your partner does or does not do. (Cue my husband and his eye rolls — because I haven't quite mastered this lesson yet.) We have had nine extra months of preparedness ahead of our partners, so take it easy on them.

The passive-aggressiveness (although super funny and more often than not makes for a good laugh with the girls) WILL NOT help (even if you feel good saying it at that moment). Our partners are doing their best; they are trying and figuring it out just as we are. Instead, be a team and divide and conquer. I know what you're all saying, 'cause I said it too: Why the hell do they have to be told or asked? Because they do. We need to stop trying to figure out the reasons behind the 'why' and start solving our own problems. Things are not getting done? Make a list. Things are not being done the way you want them to be? Teach them. They aren't offering to make dinner? Schedule it in. More often than not, they are willing to do it — but for whatever reason (and from my experience) they need to be told because they certainly will not guess.

Be honest about your expectations. Trust your partner — you chose them for a reason, so have a little faith that things will eventually get done and no one will get hurt in the process ... right?

5. The juggle is so real, Mama.

Oh Mama, there is no such thing as the perfect balance, so please stop wasting your precious time trying to achieve it (or pretending to others that you are). Trying to juggle physical health and mental health, while giving time to two new babies was tough, and something that I am still juggling daily. Just please, Mama, do what works for you and your family. Everyone else comes second, so stop trying to please everyone.

Mom guilt is so real and it never goes away. Name it, own it, talk through it. It's the internal struggle that I wrestle with daily — the guilt that someone else is raising them. The guilt that someone else is enjoying amazing moments with them. That someone else is witnessing and joining in on their milestones. Someone else gets more hugs from them. And as much as I appreciate all of the wonderful people in my children's lives for loving and caring for them as I do, they are NOT me, and therein lies the mom guilt. As mamas, we receive these mixed messages when we share that we are drained or beaten up or just simply having tough days such as, "Enjoy the tough times, they too shall pass" or "Don't blink because they'll grow up." How the hell are we supposed to NOT feel the guilt when needing a break when these messages are spewed at us daily?

It has taken me six years to say two simple words (pardon my French): FUCK IT. I cannot be there for every milestone, mistake made, boo-boo had, or memory made — it just isn't possible. But, when I am there, I am enjoying my children to the best of my ability, and they know that I love them. That right there is the only thing that matters, that my babies (even though they're six) are loved — and boy are they loved.

So remember, Mamas, you've got this. There is no right way, there is no wrong way — you just need to figure out how to make it YOUR way.

Key Takeaway

Reflect on this author's work and write down one key idea, concept, or theme that you can take with you in your own life! If something really hit home, connect with the author and get social!

....
....
....
....
....
....
....
....
....
....
....
....
....
....
....
....
....

Chapter 11
Sharana Ali

Author Photo: Liz Salzman Photography
Find Sharana: @bossinthesixedition

Thirty-something. Divorcée. Single Mother. Woman of Colour. Business Owner. Corporate World Warrior. Standing tall and proud at five feet, with my eyes always lined, brows in place, coffee in hand at 9:00 a.m., and a glass of red by 5:00 p.m. My life is far from Insta-glam or Pinterest perfect, and while I'll probably only ever be semi-money rich, in my love bank, I'm a gazillionaire.

I'm Sharana. I am the perfect cocktail of all of those adjectives above — but none of them mean more to me than the term "Mama." I've been a mama to my game-changer daughter for the last four years and nine months (pregnancy totally counts in that timeframe). From the moment I saw that bright blue plus sign, my world was rocked and there was no going back.

Of those four years, I've physically been a single mom for three. Emotionally — I was always riding the single mama roller-coaster, with each bump, whirl, and sure — the urge to throw up once in a while.

While I wouldn't say that I'm a mom-of-all-moms expert, I'd like to think that in the single mom world I've created for myself and The Game Changer, I'm getting pretty good at this motherhood thing. Granted, if you ask me tomorrow how I feel as a mom, I'll be sobbing on the floor, desiring to do more for my kid. *If this isn't motherhood, I don't know what is.*

Over the last couple of years, I've learned a thing or two. Things I wish I knew when I started this journey — or at least things I wish I heard people talk about — to normalize what it looked like to not only be a millennial mom but a divorced single millennial mom who wanted to take over the world (...world domination has always been a goal of mine). And so, I'll share what I wish I knew then.

1. Doing it all doesn't mean having it all.

I've never been good at math, but I understand that 1 + 1 = 2. It's methodical. When you add the right numbers together, you'll always get the same result. For a long time, I thought this was how life was — especially life as a mom. I figured, if I did all the feeding, changing, bathing, cooking, cleaning, entertaining, ate well, slept as little as possible, and put dinner on the table by 6:00 p.m., I would be guaranteed happiness. Cue massive wakeup call. I crashed. I did it all for all of my pregnancy and the better part of The Game Changer's first year. I wasn't happy though. I was actually nowhere close to happy, physically exhausted, and mentally broken.

Doing it all didn't mean having it all, and it's okay. Ironically, at the time I lived with someone else. Now, on my own — I actually do have it all. The definition of "all," however, has changed. I no longer need to make elaborate lunches, my kid doesn't have to eat homemade everything, I don't actually have to make her Halloween costume — I let things slide and prioritize our mental and physical health above all else.

Does the laundry pile up? Do the floors get muddy? Does the play-room look like the Tasmanian devil whipped through? Sure. But, both The Game Changer and I have never laughed as much; there has never been a greater sense of peace and happiness.

2. Single and ready to mingle.

Whether you're doing this with a partner, an army, or on your own you can do this! Two years into being a mom, I became a single mom A single mom, by choice.

Was it scary? Scarier than my worst nightmare but equally freeing and empowering at the same time. I'll never forget the first couple of days — I was living with my parents — in a house that was ful of humans yet I felt so alone. I knew I would have rather done this whole mothering thing by myself, instead of in an environment that wouldn't serve my daughter or myself. I was confident in my decision but wavered in what our family dynamic would look like.

And so, I began to talk about it. I began using social media to nor-malize being divorced, a single mom, and only in my early thirties. was ready to get back out there — and not out there in the sense o dating. But out there in the sense of reclaiming my independence now as a mother, paving the way for her daughter to be confident to walk any line she chose to.

I was ready to mingle. I was shit scared of judgment but knew wasn't the first single mom and I wouldn't be the last. I also want to make it clear that no matter what your family dynamic looks like - love, trust, and respect for yourself speaks more than two humans in a home caring for a child.

And so, if you're a single mom soldier, I not only salute you, but I commend you for putting you and your child(ren) above all else, despite what society tells us.

3. Having a village is cool, but this community is gated.

The age-old tale of it takes a village to raise a child couldn't have been truer for me. I know that I had what it took, and I could make it work on my own, but holy crap, does it feel good to know that you can take a shower and there is an extra pair of eyes on your kid.

We live with my parents. They have been my saving grace pretty much since birth, but more so after becoming a mom. Their wealth of knowledge, patience, understanding, and overall love (read: obsession) with being grandparents bode well in raising The Game Changer. Quite frankly, it also gives me the grace of balancing being a human and wanting to chase my dreams while being a mom.

Is it possible to do it without a village? Sure. Has having a village made my life a little comfier? Absolutely.

At the front of this community is a massive gate. A gate of trust, responsibility, and honesty. Not everyone is allowed beyond these iron-clad walls. I trust and respect the advice of very few, because at the end of the day — I am Mama.

So, go ahead — accept the help; rely on your community for support and guidance, but don't ever forget that they are lucky to be in your maternal circle, and ultimately your laws reign supreme.

4. Your intuition is your mama manual.

I tried to read the books — all of them. I just couldn't. I couldn't buy into the idea that a book or two could serve as universal for every mom, in every country, in every situation.

But I still craved a how-to. I still wanted some sort of reassurance. Over time, I started listening to that little voice in my heart; I started listening to the signs that my body was telling me through how it would react in different scenarios. I started relying on my intuition as my mama manual.

Is this process easy? Abso-effing-lutely not. It was all about trial and error and realizing that everything I questioned already had an answer. I just had to listen; I had to trust.

Whether you are a mom by giving birth, through surrogacy, an adoptive mom, a stepmom, a bonus mom, or a maternal figure, there's a shift in your intuition the minute your role changes. Your intuition will guide you on an individualized basis — something that no manual will ever do.

5. Your mom badge isn't taken away when you make a mistake.

Hey, guess what? While being a mom, you're also human. You're going to make mistakes, you're going to feel guilty and less than, but nothing will take away from the fact that you are the very best mom for your child, and each day you are doing as much as you can.

Just shy of one year old, The Game Changer broke her leg. It was a hairline fracture, as she played in her crib. She didn't fall out, but while trying to stand, she fell and landed on her leg.

The guilt I felt, the anger — it was palpable. The incident made me question my ability as a mother, and I kept thinking it was so careless of me. The scenario played out in my mind close to a million times, and each time — while I knew there was nothing I could have done to stop it — my heart broke because she was broken (literally).

Over time, I had to change the narrative; I wasn't a bad mom because she had broken her leg. In fact, I was a proud mom because she was confident enough to take the leap. I now joke about it, reminding parents when they say, "You can't break them"... that actually you can.

Does it make me a bad mom because 90% of the time I have no idea what I'm doing? Absolutely not! If I've learned anything through this crazy journey, it's that as much as our children are learning, they are teaching us as moms, and we are, in fact, just trying to create a balanced life together.

The good news is, there isn't a watchdog taking note of your every move. There's no right way to mother or to parent. The only way is *your way* as it fits for **you** and **your family**. That's how I'm moving forward in motherhood, and I encourage you to do the same.

Key Takeaway

Reflect on this author's work and write down one key idea, concept, or theme that you can take with you in your own life! If something really hit home, connect with the author and get social!

....

....

....

....

....

....

....

....

....

....

....

....

....

....

....

....

Chapter 12
Janelle Scannell

Author Photo: Kate Wilenski Photography
Find Janelle: @janellescannell

"Did someone say Pinot Grigio?"
I'm a girl's girl who sees the very best in each person, the wife of a hard-working stud muffin, and the momma to two incredible children. You'll find me thanking the good Lord above each night and I love putting the AWK in awkward — YUP I'm "that" person — *insert laughing face emoji*.

As much as I love living in a world of rainbows and sunshine, I have downplayed this dark cloud of shame that I carry, one that has affected me the majority of my life. I have taken my struggles and converted them into lessons, finding the right balance when my anxiety decides to make an appearance. Through trial and error, I continuously learn how to be the best version of myself. This topic is quite taboo and is one that doesn't come easy to write. As a child, I was sexually abused by my stepfather. Unsure of who to turn to, I confided in my sister. We banded together and mustered up the courage to speak up (to the most logical person one would go to), and we were unsuccessful. By unsuccessful, I mean I wasn't believed. So, I did what I thought would be best to keep the peace. I suppressed it all and continued to let it be a part of my childhood ... until I was 18 and then it was "PEACE OUT!" I believed that if I left home, the memories would stay there.

Fast forward to "K1." She is from my first marriage. Getting married young and having as many children as God wanted me to have was the plan I always had for myself. Well, when my marriage wasn't working, I had to move back home and that is when the abuse began again, but this time it was different. I had my own child to protect so I had to get out! I could not expose her to the toxic environment. The lessons mentioned, I'm still learning from. As my children grow my parenting style evolves with it.

Through my ups and downs, I have managed to take control of my anxiety and use it to my benefit as an individual, wife, and mother.

1. You've got this.

I am now married to a wonderfully supportive man and together we have a son "K2." Imagine this: a 5-year-old, a new baby, and constantly living in fear makes an interesting combo. Balancing a panic attack while potty training and trying to leave to do a school pick-up can be draining. These two depend on me for everything, so when my body starts to get hot, my vision is blurry, my heart feels like it's escaping my body and my breath is short, wanting to hide in a dark hole, as hard as it is — is not an option. The smallest thing can set me off. I can become distant and quiet. I have to pull myself out of it because my children don't deserve this part of me. My children are not the cause, so I must be patient.

I have tried different tactics, like grounding and therapy. I stopped therapy because of fear and the unknown. I know this will pass, so what I found successful when my anxiety would begin to strike was self-talk and a whole lotta patience with myself, my healing process, and with my children. As much as I want this feeling of YUCK gone, I had to understand that healing takes time and to not get discouraged when things don't go as planned. Learning to differentiate what is going on in my head versus reality is a struggle, but I need to remind myself: the creak of my bedroom door is the children coming in because they can't sleep. It's not HIM coming into my room like he frequently would. Janelle, be patient. Your kids depend on you.

2. To be or not to be... VULNERABLE.

Growing up, my family was very private. We never spoke about struggles; we certainly did not talk about IT. I think it was a pride thing. To me, I took sharing private information and sharing feelings that weren't positive as a sign of weakness, and being the person that I am — felt like a burden. With that mentality, I noticed my behaviour spilling onto my daughter where she wouldn't express her feelings, in fear of hurting another person. She would suppress it much like I did.

Something would then trigger her and she would explode with a ton of emotions and be overwhelmed not knowing how to handle it or control it. One day it happened, and I thought "OMG I'm looking in the mirror!" I have taught this little girl to hide her feelings, and that, through my own actions, everything is supposed to be perfect and we shouldn't feel or show others our sadness. Boy, was I wrong! The guilt I carried was indescribable.

That is when I changed. I vowed to change and be more raw and

real with my family, friends, most importantly, my children. I am supposed to set the example for my children and pave the path. How
could I set the example for my children and pave the path. How I'm
not being authentic?

Asking for help or asking to talk to someone has always been hard
for me. Whether it had to do with my divorce or my trauma, I felt like
a broken record. I always wanted to be sensitive to others and what
they had going on, so coming to a friend or family about it I felt selfish. I had to reflect and approach this in a different light —and that
was to be vulnerable. Showing my kids that it is okay to be vulnerable with our feelings is actually a sign of STRENGTH. It's what we as
parents want from our children; we want them to ask for our help;
we want for them to share how they feel and feel comfortable to
come to us without judgment. Which brings me to my next lesson …

3. Words, they're heavy.

By now, K1 knows that I have dealt with something in my life that has
affected me. But I have to set a standard. I have to try to raise my two
children to be accountable for their words and actions. Something as
small as telling the Ks we can get ice cream; the follow-through is so
important! It's these baby steps that have shown me that the actions
following the words can have a big impact on my children.

When I am overcome with emotions, knowing that it's my anxiety poking through, I can turn into a totally different person. As hard
as it is to admit, it's not a very pleasant side of me. I tend to be short
and standoffish, which can lead into an argument with my husband,
knowing full well it has nothing to do with him, but rather the demons
I am fighting with on the inside. It's easier said than done, but not a
single person will be able to move past anything if they don't make
the changes to better themselves or their situation. After an argument
I'd say that I was sorry, but what was I sorry for? Am I apologizing for

the sake of stopping the argument or am I saying sorry and following through with my apology by learning from my mistakes? If another argument arises will I follow the same habit or will I adjust my behaviour? Children pick up on the tension. They do hear the arguments, but it's our actions that they'll remember, and how we conduct ourselves when we are put into a certain situation. I find it so important to be accountable for your own words and actions as my words as a young child had no bearing on what actions were taken.

4. T.R.U.S.T.

Looking back, I realized that I had the wrong idea of trust. From a "parent" to my ex-husband, I thought that just because they're significant people in my life, that trust was automatic. Starting fresh had me all sorts of confused, which led me to having a hard time trusting people; it's like I went from one extreme to another.

Sharing my story was hard before motherhood. Now, as a mother sharing my story and trying to make sense of my struggle, trusting has been harder. I knew that feeling stemmed from not feeling protected as a child, so I overcompensated by being that helicopter mom. If I could control every aspect of my life, nothing bad could happen, and there'd be no one to blame but myself. The worry I had — that what happened to me could happen to my children — followed me everywhere. So, with that mindset, I had a hard time even trusting myself. Did that sometimes cloud my vision and cause me to miss out on the beauty of being a mother? It did — 100%. It has taken a while, but I had to learn to trust by putting myself out there and fighting past the fear. I had to put myself in situations to help me regain that trust in people. I also had to trust that the skills I have been teaching my children would resonate with them. Breaking the mold of "I'm the parent, you're the child, so listen to what I say" is a fine line because yes, we know what's best for our little ones, but they are individuals and we have to listen to what affects them and how things make them feel. As a parent, As a parent, I have to trust not only my gut but, my children's as well.

5. You will never go away.

This is for you, the one that haunts me daily. You may have had an impact on my life but you do not control it. I know the love I have to give. The "love" you gave me was not love at all; it was selfish and a poor excuse to satisfy your bad behaviour. I know the innocence you took from me and that is something I will not let my children lose. Through the years I have spent many days sad, many nights afraid and over-thinking worst-case scenarios. I see that it was unhealthy and con-sumed so much of my time, time taken away from my family. Yes, I suffer from PTSD and anxiety but that does not define who I am.

There came a time when I said, "Enough is enough, I'm at my wits' end!" That does not mean that I have healed completely; it means that I have built up enough strength to keep pushing forward. I have accepted what has happened to me and I strive to use it to better myself because I shouldn't be ashamed. It took recognizing that YOU were the root of my struggles. Without that, I wouldn't have been able to see the issue and take the steps that I needed to. If it weren't for my children watching me and keeping me motivated, I wouldn't have found that strength to be a voice to the voiceless. There still will be days that I take five steps backward, but I will appreciate each of those days and know that I am in charge of what I make of those days or how much I will let it take from me. Sometimes bad things happen, but it's how we react to situations that determine what kind of outcome we'll get.

My hope is to bring comfort to other mommas who have gone through this. I know it can be debilitating at times, and the climb back up is not easy, but I promise it's worth it. We all have our crosses to carry; Jesus did and Simon was there to help him! I'm humbled to be a part of this — and I am here for YOU!

God bless,

X

Key Takeaway

Reflect on this author's work and write down one key idea, concept, or theme that you can take with you in your own life! If something really hit home, connect with the author and get social!

Chapter 13
Grace Valentini

Author Photo: Rick Denham Photography
Find Grace: @grace_valentini17

"When I grow up I'm having four kids!"
I will have my boys first and then my girl, so the brothers will protect her. All I want is to be a mom! This is my 11-year-old self in Grade 6, at recess, sitting on the portable step telling my friends how my life would be.

Guess what? I did have my two boys and a daughter many years later, however, the universe had different plans for me when it came to how my life as a mother would turn out.

My marriage ended after 17 years and my relationship with my boys changed forever. They became the "men of the house" and took on many roles within our relationship.

Michael, being the oldest, dealt with a lot of the emotional, ugly truths of divorce. Joseph took care of all the household things I didn't know how to do, while also taking care of his younger sister. Victoria became my sidekick and still is to this day because she was at the tender age of almost two when we divorced.

Some things have never changed that I wanted for my children. I struggled in school and dropped out of college three times, never getting a diploma, so getting an education was paramount. I wanted my children to know how smart they were and that anything was possible!

I was an overweight child and never played sports, so my children were going to be healthy and 100% were going to play organized sports! I married young and had the children I always wanted but never pursued my dreams. I wanted to make sure that my children pursued their dreams, traveled the world, and squeezed everything out of life. I wanted them to know that there is such a thing as do-overs, nothing is a mistake, and you can always start over, no matter how difficult.

My name is Grace and I'm a mom several times over. I have a 26-year-old named Michael; he started my journey to self-discovery, and I feel we grew up alongside each other. My 23-year-old, Joseph, propelled me on my weight loss journey. My 14-year-old daughter Victoria is a girl I've always wanted to be. She is everything I wasn't; a do-over of the unconfident struggling young girl I was. I'm remarried to an amazing man named Dino, and I'm a stepmom to Alyssa, 23, Maddalena, 14, and Dino Jr., 12. They came into my life to give me the big family I've always wanted.

People always say that being a mother is all unicorns and rainbows, but I soon discovered that there is more to motherhood than I was really prepared for. Each child played a role in who I am today with their different personalities and the love we share.

I am currently in the process of finishing my certification to become a consultant with the Proctor Gallagher Institute and having my gratitude journal published. My passions are health, exercising, the laws of the universe, and manifesting.

These are my lessons in no particular order...

1. DO NOT live vicariously through your children.

You might have their whole life planned out for them, you may want them to have everything — the awards, the recognition, and the abundance you never had. You want to make sure that they don't make the same mistakes you made or suffer in any way. You know anything is possible for them and you will do anything to help them realize their dreams. Unfortunately, they might have different plans that don't resemble your visions. That's okay because what you really want is to raise good humans. In the end, you will realize, that's all that really matters, and all the small stuff you worried about means nothing. If they follow their passions they will do well and be happy. As a mom, that's all we really want for our children.

2. Actions speak louder than words... and they are always listening.

Your children are always watching and listening to what you do and even start to imitate you unconsciously. If you are kind, they will be; if you lead a healthy lifestyle, they will follow. The saying, "The apple doesn't fall far from the tree." — It's true. They absorb so much information at a young age that will stay with them for life. Being who I am today, I would never have those intense adult conversations (financial, emotional, etc.) in front of my children. Let's be real, sometimes we are not consciously aware that the kids are listening. The car rides, the dinners, the in-betweens — kids are sponges and they internalize everything! They don't need the details of your life money issues, or your unhappiness. Let them be kids. They have their whole lives to worry about adult things. There is no need to burden them now.

3. You will not always be their "Number 1."

If you are looking down at your perfect little baby right now, I know you're saying, "Not my child!" Yes, your child that you carried for nine months, that you would die for, will dislike you at some point for something. It can be very easy to cross the line between motherhood to friendship, and I struggled with this one because I wanted to be close to my children and know what's going on in their lives. I always wanted them to come to me as an outlet for them, whether good or bad. When you cross that line, it becomes harder to give consequences for their actions. My dad always told me that a branch is formed when the tree grows, just like a child.

Behaviour is formed at a young age. Start young because it's harder to backtrack when they are used to getting away with things. Motherhood is not perfect. We only do what we know at the time. Don't beat yourself down. Motherhood is a challenging job — who cares if you're not number one, you're doing your job! You can't do everything right, (which is impossible) but you will be blamed for everything gone wrong in their lives!

4. They will always love the other parent.

Coming from divorce, this was a difficult lesson because I thought "I" was doing everything right, not their dad. In the eyes of a child, no matter what, they love both parents equally, as it should be. A child learns from both parents and equally needs the love of a mom and dad. A child's needs always have to come first, above your own ego. There was a lot of personal development to make this realization. I divorced their dad, they didn't!

5. Make time for you, your relationship, and stop feeling guilty.

Let's talk about guilt, for real! You love your children more than anything — Mother Nature made it that way — but you feel guilty if you leave them, guilty if you want time for yourself, and then there's the guilt you get when you look at other moms who seem to have it all together. Their kids are well dressed, well behaved, read all the books, are extremely athletic, super smart, and just well-rounded. There is no perfect — so STOP comparing! Stay in your lane and do the best you can with what you know, until you know better.

Go out and recharge with other humans or do the things you enjoyed before becoming a mother. Feed your soul and fill your cup. Your children will thank you.

We forget about our relationships as well, especially during the first year of a child's life. The more children we have, the more we put our relationship with our partner on the back burner. It's so important to keep the spark alive because no child wants to live in a home with unhappy parents. They would much rather see you both happy and showing affection, even though they think it's gross. Remember why you fell in love and had this beautiful child. Be a team and stick together and never disagree on something in front of the children. Your marriage will be better for it.

If you remember anything from my chapter, PLEASE burn this in your mind: It's true, the years go by so fast, like the blink of an eye. If you are a new mom and you're exhausted, your nipples hurt, you think you've lost the vagina you once had, it's all good. Everything goes back to some kind of normalcy. What you don't get back are those years that you think are SO hard and you can't wait for your kids to get older so you can have some freedom.

One day, you truly will look back and think, those were the best years. When you think you are too busy, make the time to read that extra book. When you think you are too tired to watch another Disney movie, do it anyway. When you think you have to make dinner and clean the house and you can't play outside anymore, get takeout. You will have lots of time to get your body back, to make money, to organize, and get your life back. But I promise you, nothing is more important than the TIME that you have with your kids! It is so precious. Make it great.

Have NO REGRETS!

P.S.

· Yes, the baby will always be spoiled.

· There is such a thing as "middle child syndrome."

· The oldest does get the brunt of it.

I love being a mom <3[1]

---

[1] Texting lingo <3 means ♥

Key Takeaway

Reflect on this author's work and write down one key idea,
concept, or theme that you can take with you in your own life! If
something really hit home, connect with the author and get social!

....
....
....
....
....
....
....
....
....
....
....
....
....
....
....
....
....
....

Chapter 14

Nikki King

Author Photo: Stephanie Webster Photography
Find Nikki: @nikkikingfit

Motherhood was never something that I felt was for me. From a very young age, I was convinced that I would never be able to — or want to — have children. I can vividly remember sitting in sex education class, mortified to learn how babies were made.

"You put what in the what now?! No ... Nah uh ... That's insane — I'm never having kids."

I can just imagine my parents' relief, knowing I hadn't the slightest interest in sex, let alone one day having a baby of my own.

It wasn't until college that I revisited the idea. I was in a serious relationship with the guy I would one day marry, and my period was late. One day on my lunch break at work, I mustered up the courage to buy myself a pregnancy test. No one was aware, other than me. Taking the test was scary as fuck. I had waited to do the test on a day when I knew that I'd be up visiting my boyfriend at his university, but also a day when I knew that I'd be alone in his dorm for chunks of the day because he had class.

Those three minutes that I had to wait for the result felt like an eternity, but I'll never forget the feeling when I saw those two pink lines glaring back at me.

I kept tight-lipped about my little secret for days. Scared that if I told anyone, I would be judged and made to feel like a failure. We took every proper precaution to prevent pregnancy, and it failed us. We were the 2% that fell victim to ineffective contraception. It can happen to anyone.

My dirty little secret was eventually made known to my boyfriend. I poured my heart out to him about two weeks later when I miscarried. It was a very difficult conversation to have, but as a couple, we grew stronger because of it. It allowed us to discuss our plans for the future, and openly communicate our desires for future family planning. He was very aware that I had a lot of unease about becoming a mother. That never went away.

My firstborn was born in 2009.

The journey into motherhood is fucking scary. Rewarding, oh-so-rewarding, but scary as hell. Just when you think you have motherhood all figured out, someone comes along and shakes the snow globe and your whole world becomes discombobulated again. Motherhood is a constant learning curve that no one can prepare you for. There are a lot of hiccups in the road, but it can be one of the most blissfully chaotic adventures — if you let it be.

My name is Nicole, mother of four, doer-of-all-things, wannabe culinary expert, nature lover, and Certified Personal Trainer who is having a secret love affair with poutine ...and these are some of the lessons I've learned so far in motherhood:

1. You can't prevent the hard, scary days.

But what you can do is trust your instincts.

It's so easy to want to be at your child's beck and call. I feel like at some point we all feel somewhat like a helicopter parent. The world is a scary place, and it can be a difficult feat to break free from the chains and allow our kids to have a little bit of independence.

I have had the privilege of being a work-at-home mom since my oldest daughter was a toddler. We live in a small town, which means our home school isn't in close proximity to our house. Realistically, I could have driven my daughter to school each day, but her heart was set on taking the big yellow school bus. Imagine my heart on her first day of Kindergarten when she flat out refused to let me drop her off.

She was taking the bus, whether I liked it or not. She was a big girl now after all. The first few days went well, and I started to feel more okay with our decision...

Until that one afternoon that the bus arrived at the stop, and watched all the kids at our stop deboard — all except my 4-year-old daughter. The bus drove off and I just stood there, 16 weeks pregnant with a toddler in tow — paralyzed with fear. Panic consumed every inch of me.

A local high schooler who recognized me, let me know she was going to run a block up and flag down the bus driver at his next stop. When I arrived at the stop, the bus driver immediately got the school on the phone. The administrators were insistent that my daughter was on the bus, claiming that she was tired and that she must have fallen asleep. I can't even tell you how many times I had to climb aboard the vehicle to keep confirming the fact that my daughter was nowhere to be found, and no one could tell me where she was. It was my worst nightmare. It's every parent's worst nightmare.

I had every possible worst-case scenario running through my

head. A sobbing mess standing on the street corner with passersby not knowing what to do other than to offer a sympathetic look, not being fully aware of the situation at hand.

It took almost an hour and a half for them to locate my daughter. She had been placed on the wrong school bus and attempted to get off the bus at the last stop on that bus driver's route. Thank god this driver had some wits about her and quickly realized that my daughter wasn't one of her bus students and stopped her from getting off the bus.

"Mommy, I didn't know where I was... I was going to get off to look for you."

Words that will forever haunt me.

No one ever took accountability or offered an apology for the incident that unfolded that day, but I made damn sure that the school put proper protocols in place to ensure that this would never happen again.

The following school day? Well, let's just say that she took the bus again. I really didn't want her to, but I knew it was in her best interest. My hands were tied. I couldn't let the hard and scary days in motherhood infiltrate her with fear of the unknown, especially when it hadn't really fazed her at all.

2. Screen time is not the all-time enemy.

Let me repeat that. You are not a horrible parent for allowing your kid to have screen time. You are also not a horrible parent for glancing at your phone for a few minutes here and there over the day.

Screen time is not the all-time enemy. Does that mean that I allow my kids to be on their devices all day long? Absolutely not. I have boundaries, but at the end of the day, some days they do end up on their devices more than others. I have no guilt for that. It buys me time to get shit done around the house that I may not have otherwise readily been able to do. It buys me a little bit of solace on the days when I want nothing more than to pull out my hair or bury my head in a pillow and scream.

And for the love of god — next time you see a Mom at the park quickly glancing at her phone or scrolling Facebook ... cut her some slack. You really don't know what her day has looked like up until then. It may be her only way of evading the disconnect and void that motherhood can often cause us to feel when we're at home raising these tiny little clones of ours.

Let's stop the Mom-shaming. Please!

3. "This Too shall pass."

But what happens when it doesn't?

Growth spurts, sleepless nights, the fucking fours (oh my god ... the fucking fours, am I right?)

The moments that no one truly prepares you for. The days you want nothing more than to crawl back into that blanket fort and quit adulting for life. It's on those days that it can all feel so isolating, so overwhelming. It's important to remember, during these seasons, that you're not alone. Most of these phases are just that ...phases. They will pass just as quickly as the ocean current changes.

One thing you will never hear me tell another mother is the phrase, "this too shall pass." It's a phrase that, in my opinion, gets thrown around all too loosely.

Just imagine that mom friend of yours, reaching out and confiding in you that she is really struggling. Yes, the things that she is confiding to you could all be a "normal" part of this motherhood experience. But what if there is that whole other layer? You know the one ... the darkness ... the anxiety ... the depression. There is such a stigma behind talking about your mental health, and it can take a lot for someone to cry for help.

There have been moments in motherhood where I have never felt more alone, claustrophobic, and out of control. These are the moments that don't pass as easily. It's a struggle that I have been dealing with for

11 years now, and that's okay. It's important to recognize these harder seasons. More so, it's just as important to understand that you don't have to weather these never-ending storms alone. There are many great resources you can access and people you can reach out to for help, me included.

You are not alone.

4. There's only one of you in life.

Make sure that you take care of yourself. Plain and simple.

For the longest time, I was afraid to leave the house. To take time away and do things just for myself. What if my baby needed me?

I'd get invited out to girls' nights and I would get myself so worked up that I'd actually allow the worry to convince me that I couldn't do these things. So, I'd cancel. I'd cancel often. You could say postpartum anxiety was partially to blame for this behaviour. Anxiety is the ultimate BFF, your one and only, who you can always rely on to tell you why you can't do something. Filling your mind with so much clutter and unnecessary worry, it can be hard to shut it off. Sadly, my wake-up call was when my friends stopped calling, stopped inviting me out ... life moved on without me in the picture. It was a hard pill to swallow that hurt. It hurt a lot, but it was the wake-up call that I needed.

The reality is that your baby can survive a few hours without you (and you will survive too, Mama!).

Create the habit of making time for girls' nights, going to get your hair done, attending therapy sessions, enjoying a car ride alone while singing your heart out to cheesy oldies-but-goodies (a lil' MMMBop never hurt anyone!) ... whatever your self-care routine looks like, practice it. Make it a daily exercise. You will be a better Mom for it!

As one of my favourite quotes reads:

"You were someone before you were their mom, remember that."

5. You do you, Boo.

Could you imagine if we all conformed to the ideals that "parenting experts" mold us into thinking we should be? NO — because it's not fucking realistic.

The whole world is full of these parenting gurus. You know the ones who claim to have all their shit together. As if you can just buy a book on parenting and rely on it as the ultimate fix-all.

According to the books, I'm doing this parenting thing all wrong. Imagine if I actually let those books define me? I'd be one hot mess.

If it's not those experts you need to worry about, then it's living up to the expectations of others. Nothing is better than when a childless person chastises your way of parenting, as if they can do it better.

But you know what?

At the end of the day, I am doing my best. That's all you can really do in this journey through motherhood. There is no right or wrong way. Just trust your instincts. They are a great guide, and they're usually right, too.

The best thing you can do is love your kids. Trust the process. Make them feel safe and supported. Teach them not to grow up to be little assholes. Everything else will come with time.

There's no predicting how your days will unfold, and some days will be harder than others. That's the messy beautiful truth behind motherhood though. It's one big life lesson, and each one of us is on our own adventure. I could sit here all day and spout off lesson after lesson that I've learned along the way. Some might be more relatable than others. Those that aren't relatable doesn't mean that either one of us has it any better or easier. We are all living a different story. Support one another, be kind, and keep that judgmental catty bullshit to yourself.

Motherhood takes a village.

And in case no one has told you lately, I'm so proud of you!

Key Takeaway

Reflect on this author's work and write down one key idea, concept, or theme that you can take with you in your own life! If something really hit home, connect with the author and get social!

....
....
....
....
....
....
....
....
....
....
....
....
....
....
....
....
....
....

#5lessons #leadherpublishing

Chapter 15
Laura Vesel

Find Laura: @lauraves_fitness

I always wanted a family of my own. My goals and expectations were to go to university, get a job, get a husband, buy a house (with a dog!), do a bunch of amazing things, and then have TWO children.

Motherhood was always a goal, however, it came to me in a very unexpected order. At the age of twenty-four, a relatively new university grad and working as a health club manager and just securing our first apartment together, we found out we were expecting our first daughter

My ten-year plan became a 10-month plan, in an instant. Beyond confident in our ability to raise a child but still terrified of all the unknowns and adapting at every step to make it work, I wouldn't change a moment.

In the past eleven years, we were married (with our daughter in our arms), purchased our first home, and then built our forever home … oh and now we have a total of THREE beautiful daughters (we were on a roll!)

I still have a passion for health and wellness. I am a certified fitness instructor and fitness coach, but I now have a responsibility far greater as a stay-at-home mother.

Through coaching and health and wellness, I am able to help people of all walks of life empower themselves to continually evolve, grow, and find value in their own light while appreciating all that they have to offer.

And sometimes, I even take my own advice.

This is the only option when you have three sets of beautiful eyes watching your every move.

So that's me! I'm not an author, nor a blogger (I don't even own a journal), and my primary writing experience comes in the form of long-winded social media posts, but I am so excited for this new forum to continue creating a positive impact for those around me. Here are my 5 Lessons Learned.

1. Parenting and marriage is not a 50/50 deal.

I grew up with a wonderful nuclear family. My dad worked full-time and mom was home with us full-time until I was about nine, when she gradually returned to work over the next few years. I had always felt that both my mom and dad contributed their time and efforts equally and felt that they had figured out and upheld that unicorn parenting concept of sharing the responsibilities 50/50. So — please imagine my extreme shock (and impending resentment) after six years of marriage, a few house moves and renovations, and three babies that left me feeling like I was giving 100% … ALL.THE.TIME. Tell me if any of this feels painfully familiar: with a 5-year-old, a 3-year-old, and a fiery newborn, I was typically emotionally and physically empty by 9:00 a.m. Also important to note: my husband was probably pretty offended by my perspective that I was doing 100% of the "work," while he traveled to remote parts of the world, worked 12-hour days, mowed the lawn, cleaned the pool, and planned adventure walks (not for his personal enjoyment, to be clear).

Coming up to my eldest daughter's eleventh birthday, I have now learned that parenting requires a 100/100 commitment (and if there are more people involved in raising those babes, they also have to give 100%). We are both incomplete and unique people with our own strengths and weaknesses that typically complement each other (which is presumably why we decided to take on this crazy journey). The 100% of my ability to filter out background noise … is INCREDIBLY inadequate for success; my husband's ability to block out everything… is AMAZING. Together, our skills come together to provide our children with what they require. My husband needs 100% of my ability to slow down and breathe to complement his desire to "do." So, yes, you will feel like you are giving 100%, but you must be sure to open your eyes to the gift you are receiving from others participating in your children's upbringing, because they are also giving 100%. The key to finding truth is opening your eyes and trusting the value of your partner's 100% effort, even though it might look different than yours.

2. Anyone can have an opinion; find your own voice.

Three girls — who will become three women — each with unique abilities, strengths, and interests that will grow to form their opinions. Girl moms often hear this: "Oooh THREE girls? There must be a LOT of opinions in your house!" And to be honest, I'm guilty of that narrative too.

Webster's Dictionary defines opinion as: 1) Belief based on experience and on certain facts but not amounting to sure knowledge; 2) A judgment about a person or a thing.

Being new (or veteran) mothers, we are no strangers to opinions. From everyone. On everything. There are no shortages of opinions on every aspect of our parenting and on the behaviour of our children. Not one of those times in the grocery store checkout when someone felt the need to give me THEIR opinion did I think, "Wow! How had I not thought of that in this instance?"

I've learned that ANYONE can have an opinion, share one, or pass judgement, but what IMPACT will that have? I have learned that I need to encourage myself (and model for my girls and all women) to create meaningful impact by using my voice. Beyond sharing opinions, we need to tap into the definition of voice that embraces a "means of expression" or the "right to express a wish."

Without learning how to use our voice, our opinions (or lessons) are useless. Through sharing our experiences and value, we can make an impact on those around us. This has been one of the most powerful and life-altering realizations I have ever embraced. Through my fitness and wellness members, to my peers or other moms, I am learning the value of sharing my voice with others. I am learning every day how to do this more effectively, and I am so grateful for the opportunities it opens.

3. Elsa nailed it. I've gotta just "let it go."

I have ALWAYS had firm beliefs and held strong opinions about how things SHOULD be done (ask my mom ... to this day, we can't discuss using a dryer for laundry. Those wounds are deep). When an action falls outside of my expectations, it is not easy for me to accept. I had adopted an I'll-just-do-it-myself attitude so that life was done "right." When my life expanded to include my girls and lots of outside assistance, shit hit the fan. Even when my husband tries to pack for the kids, make their lunches, or dress them (you get it), it would put my anxiety into hyperdrive. But someone outside of my "approved circle" and oh goodness ... buckle up!

I never relinquished control when my first two were little. I held on to, "I can do it!" for dear life. When I went away, I made BOOKLETS ... with an index! Outlining exactly what and how to do "daily life," and I was STILL in knots the whole time.

When our third daughter was born, my two older girls were with my sister-in-law and my in-laws and the day they were arranged to be brought home, I suffered lots of all that "amazingness" that happens after a traumatic birth (my placenta was officially delivered on a different day than my daughter!). I panicked. Not because my insides were falling out at home, but because my in-law's booklet only included up to that day. HOW WOULD THEY ALL SURVIVE THE DAY AFTER THE BOOKLET ENDS?

That day... that was the day that I had to make the choice to "let it go." My mother-in-law has two grown children, has run a public health unit, and owns a washing machine. I had to accept that being in control at that moment was going to cause me more harm than good.

Now, this isn't something I have officially learned. I'll put this in the category of "still learning." However, I have come to realize that working my ass off to be the "do-er" was not making me feel any better.

have also found ways to allow this "let it go" mentality to serve other areas of my life. Instead of internalizing those pesky opinions from others, I just watch those suckers fly up and away as bubbles into the sun (where they burn).

So thanks, Elsa! Not only did you confirm that the sister relationship is the most important one that my girls will have, but you've also given me the gift of peace (out!).

4. Laughter is the best medicine... especially when directed at yourself.

From VERY early on in your mama journey (often during pregnancy before you even know what is coming), you will find that you have two options: laugh or cry. Throwing up in your car and bringing the bag into work ... laugh or cry. Huge wet circles on your boobs at the grocery store ... laugh or cry. In the beginning, I chose to cry. A lot. Every new situation I was put in seemed to come with some kind of humiliation at my expense and it wore at my self-worth.

As my confidence slowly built up and I was able to find a semi-normal sleep pattern, my perspective began to shift, and I began to see humility and then hilarity in my situation. In what other possible context can you live, when you have explosive poop on your shirt, or small (yet strangely loud!) voice pointing out the zit you picked at in a line-up full of people — that shit is pretty funny.

Laughter diffuses almost all negative feelings and lightens incredibly heavy spaces, and motherhood and parenting is about as heavy as it gets. There will never be a day that you don't experience a sense of failure, and if you choose to cry, you can get stuck there. If you choose to laugh, you create the power to shift the dynamic.

So, be silly! If dinner is a shit show, stand on your chair and dance. Post that ridiculous picture your sister took showing your worst an-

gle as your husband tries to make you kiss a fish (laugh or cry, right?).
Create a joyful experience for you and those around you. If not to
save your sanity, choose laughter because your children deserve to
see and feel you experiencing joy.

5. The true meaning of strength in motherhood is the ability to be soft.

The idea of "mother empowerment" usually hinges on the idea of
being strong. It's actually a very popular catchphrase screened onto
any and all kinds of pieces of apparel, but in my opinion, when it
comes to motherhood, the traditional qualities of strength do not
apply. Let me explain.

Strength in motherhood requires you to be soft; to survive the ups
and downs and constant changes. We must be able to easily mold,
fold, and bend. We cannot simply be able to withstand force and
pressure over an extended period of time; we must be able to move
with and around the pressures we face every day from our children,
our spouses, and most importantly, the view we form and hold of
ourselves.

As women, to be truly strong, we must be able to open our hearts
to experience and make space for the hard times. To sustain our
selves over the lifetime of our family, strength will come from you
ability to accept the hard, not hold up against it. Once you've accept
ed that there is a force working negatively, you can adapt and take
control to manoeuvre through it.

Resistance and willpower are finite concepts. Both will eventually
run out.

But, the ability to embrace and acknowledge the hard times and
move through them with flexible strength — that will sustain and
regenerate.

Key Takeaway

Reflect on this author's work and write down one key idea,

concept, or theme that you can take with you in your own life! If

something really hit home, connect with the author and get social!

Chapter 16
Teri Canestraro

Author Photo: Sarah Singleton
Find Teri: @tcancans @femaleswhosidehustle

Let me start by saying — thank you in advance for reading and your understanding. Being a mom is one of the most gratifying titles, but at times, it is also the scariest whirlwind of experiences. So, feeling safe to share my views and to be vulnerable with my thoughts is an incredible opportunity.

Okay, let's get real and raw — motherhood is crazy! Crazy scary, crazy joyful, crazy exhausting, crazy rewarding, and the list goes on. I cannot distinctly remember knowing that I wanted to be a mom. I did not dream about it or obsess over it — I just figured that once I got married, it was the next natural step.

My journey to motherhood started out "textbook." I fell in love, got married, practiced the birds and the bees, and then wham bam thank you, ma'am! Easy peasy pregnancy, but a hell of a labour story — saving some details but *she* is reconstructed and gnarly. After that, life was pretty chill and almost Hallmark movie-like — then we wanted Baby #2. This period of my life tested every fibre in my body.

INFERTILITY. This rocked my world and legitimately changed who I am today. I became obsessed with it and NEEDED it to happen. At this point, for reasons I cannot explain, I somehow was NOT okay with having only one child. My project-based, goal-oriented, need things in my control, planner soul that always made what I wanted to happen, could not fathom the thought there was nothing I could do. This situation was out of my control. But five miscarriages, one diagnosed chromosome issue and one round of IVF with two separate transfers later — we got pregnant with Baby #2.

Before our reality of secondary infertility, I was the typical girl who looked confident, but I truly was not. I never talked to my girlfriends about my period, never shared anything personal at all, felt very uncomfortable in many normal situations and most times looked like I had it all together. Well, I looked back at her and realized — I was not living to my fullest potential.

Something in me changed. As hard as that period in my life was — I can look back and be grateful; of course, for my complete family, but also for the person I have become. If it wasn't for that time in my life, my chapter in this amazing book, amongst other things, would not exist, simply because I would have NEVER shared my thoughts and realities with anyone, ever.

So here we go! This is me — Teri! I am 36 years young, Mama of two miracle babies (Evan, 8, and Olivia, 2), and wife to Justin, my biggest fan and cheerleader. I hope you enjoy my five lessons.

1. Have rules... but not too many!

I am a rule follower through and through. So of course, I parent that way. Don't do this, don't do that. Do it like THIS, NOT like THAT! Use your manners. Wait your turn. Why are you doing it like that? I look back and feel bad for my son. I was consistently forcing an excessive number of rules on him. He was my first — how was I supposed to know?! I never got the MOM manual when I left the hospital. I guess it got lost in the mail!

Of course, I battle with myself. If I didn't have those rules and enforce them every damn time — would he be as kind, polite, courteous, and as well behaved? I don't know. But what I do know, is that my second child made quite a few of my rules go exploding into thin air. Best disappearing act I have ever seen. I think it might have been a combination of the new me as a mom and her being the classic "doesn't give a f**k second child." And so far, she is turning out pretty great as well!

Lesson learned after eight years of motherhood — stay firm on the core rules — don't pick your nose without a tissue, don't talk back, chew with your mouth closed. But everything will be just fine without ALL the rules I want to enforce. Wear the rainboots with your shorts in the middle of summer and eat the snack in the middle of the trampoline; all will be just fine.

2. Remember to be a kid.

I am not the mom that sits and plays for hours on end. I never made sensory bins. I never taught them every nursery rhyme, dance or song. I never made the right sounds of the trucks or animals or characters. I never cut their snacks into cute shapes. I started a business on my first maternity leave and hustled hard. I worked long days and tried to balance everything the best that I could. Then I changed careers and was hit with our infertility journey. At times, I feel like my son got short-changed. When I think back to his early years, I cannot remember much. I know we made memories — picnics, boat rides, zoo visits, and camping trips — but I don't remember just being a kid with him: sitting on the floor playing farm and zoo animals, talking about silly things under a couch fort, or laughing at the fart noises we can make on our arms. I am talking about the everyday memories.

That being said — I never did that stuff with my 2-year-old either, until now. Something recently just clicked, and I have been challenging myself to be more of a kid for my kids. I HIGHLY recommend it! The emails can wait, social media will always have content to get sucked into, you will still get dinner done on time, and that laundry will one day fold itself (right?). Being a kid for your kids truly is good for your soul. You easily forget your anxieties for a moment; whatever you were stressed about takes a back seat, and for me — I just feel all-around better and calmer.

3. Stop jumping to conclusions.

Sometimes it is incredibly difficult to always remember that they are, in fact, smart, capable humans. We teach them so much constantly and consistently that it is hard to realize when they are learning things on their own and in their own way. Take for example — toilet training. I distinctly remember (because it just happened as I'm writing this chapter — ha!) hovering over my daughter Day 4 into toilet training. Do you have to go pee? Nope! Do you have to go poo? Nope! But she is doing the funky monkey dance and I just cannot figure her out. She runs to the toilet sits, nothing. Gets up, five minutes later runs back over to the toilet, sits, nothing. This repeats about four times.

I INSTANTLY get on Google: Why is my 2-year-old saying she has to pee, going to the toilet and not peeing! I go down the rabbit hole — children's diabetes, bladder infection, UTI — like why the F**K do we do this (or really, is it just me)?

You know what it was — HER FIRST TOILET POOP! WHY COULD I NOT JUST STAY CALM AND NOT JUMP TO CONCLUSIONS? I do this with a lot of milestones and situations. OMG — why isn't she eating? Why is she waking up in the middle of the night still? Why does he still need a nap?

Lesson learned: Try not to jump to conclusions to fix and find the solutions to their every move. They are finding their groove. And it is a beautiful thing to be a part of.

4. Who they are VS. who you want them to be.

This lesson is still a battle for me.

You want the best for your child(ren). Always. And I know most of us would do anything to make that happen. But one thing I am learning that you cannot really change is WHO THEY ARE. This is such a hard concept for me to grasp. As Moms, we get to teach them and 'shape' them in so many ways yet they will still do it their own way. Which is amazing, because come to think of it — I do things my own way and am proud and grateful that I can — so should I not be teaching them that also?

We cannot change or force them to like or play a certain sport, like certain foods, be a certain gender, be attracted to a certain gender, get the "good" jobs, be interested in our favourite hobbies or activities and the list goes on. I have learned to guide rather than steer. Guiding them is more effective than steering them. I have learned to show them boundaries and the hard lines not to cross. But how they move within those boundaries is, I am coming to terms with, their choice.

If I always steer their ship, they will never get the sensations: when to slow down, when to stop, when to pivot, and when to let go. They need to understand these feelings to survive in this crazy world. It is truly a proud parent moment when you see them own who they are and have the confidence to be who they are.

5. Your spark

This lesson is a little different. This one is about you. Let's face it — things change when you become a mom. Your focus shifts and instantly you become a selfless guardian of tiny humans. The thought of jumping in front of a car to save them becomes so real. You constantly want to take their hurt and tears away. When they are sick and in pain — you wish it were you, not them. And if it were physically possible to do those things, we would in a heartbeat. In some ways, all that serve and protect Mama Bear beast mode leaves us not recognizing ourselves in the mirror.

All the needs of everyone around you start to consume you and you sometimes lose the ability to speak to your inner you. Your spark. Where does it go? The good news is, it never leaves you — she just goes into super deep hibernation for a bit until you realize that she has been sleeping for too long. WAKE HER UP! Your spark is you. Your hopes, wants, dreams, hustle, originality, and self-love live in your spark.

This is just my belief, but I think mom guilt has something to do with why our spark finds a back seat so quickly. My goal to navigate through my motherhood journey moving forward is to have a healthy balance of mom guilt and letting my spark shine. I know that my kids see me shining and working on my dreams. My hope is that it gives them the confidence to do the same. I feel like it is one of those lessons you teach them, sometimes without any words, just actions.

They will observe and learn.

Key Takeaway

Reflect on this author's work and write down one key idea,

concept, or theme that you can take with you in your own life! If

something really hit home, connect with the author and get social!

....

....

....

....

....

....

....

....

....

....

....

....

....

....

....

....

....

....

....

Chapter 17

Chelsey Mater

Author Photo: Laryssa Leigh Photography
Find Chelsey: @chelseymater

Dirt bikes, trucks, mud, and all the mess. This is my life. On top of kissing booboos, making 10 meals a day (in hopes that someone will eat SOMETHING), breaking up fights, asking, "Are you listening?" on repeat, and singing never-ending Blippi songs in my head.

My name is Chelsey and I am a boy mom to two perfect humans ages one and three. And by perfect, I mean, they are mine and I love them more than life itself, but they may actually be the death of me.

My entire life I had dreamed about being a mom. When I was a child, I had this super creepy life-like doll that I would carry around everywhere with me and pretend she was the real deal. I changed her diapers regularly and I think I even attempted to breastfeed her at one point (that's normal right?). Man, this motherhood thing is easy! Clearly, I was naive to think that there were any similarities between that life less creepy doll and bringing a screaming tiny human into existence.

When the time finally came to start trying for a family, I was devastated to learn that I wasn't ovulating and the chances of us having a baby of our own were slim. It took us 2.5 years of doctor's appointments, specialists, acupuncture visits, and disappointment before we finally got pregnant naturally. We did it! The next step is pure bliss, right?! Well, sort of.

Motherhood did NOT come naturally to me (isn't it supposed to?). I was weighed down heavily with postpartum depression (which I largely kept to myself), breastfeeding was terrifying and painful, and to top it off, my baby had to have been one of the most unhappy babies on the planet. Thank goodness for his health though, because that's all that really matters, isn't it? I think being told this made me feel all the guilt when complaining or feeling anything but happiness and love towards my new human and life. So I'll sneak in a quick pre-lesson and say, "It's okay to not be okay."

It was a rough first year into momma-hood with a roller-coaster of emotions, and just as things were getting easier, out pops baby number two!

What a difference this baby was, right from the point of conceiving (which took us no time at all). But the funny thing is, even after two years of experience, I still had no freaking clue what I was doing. Does anyone though?

Fifteen months later, with two crazy, busy, messy, hilarious little boys, I can say that I have learned quite a bit along the way.

Here is just a fraction of what I have to share:

1. You are number one.

I know what you're thinking, "But my baby is my #1!" I get it. We all love our babies more than life itself. But the truth is, when you are constantly filling everyone else's cup but your own, not only is it going to directly affect your happiness, but it will indirectly affect your children's. Kids feed off our energies, and when tension is high or fulfillment is low, they feel it.

I know I'm not the only mom who is guilty of neglecting my health. For a while, my kids took up all of my focus and energy so that I completely lost the desire to work out (which was my passion), eating became a mental escape, sleep was a distant memory, and socializing consisted of baby talk and answering 500 toddler questions. Too much of this for anyone is bound to take a toll on your physical and mental health. And on top of that, when your life becomes all about your kids, do you know what else suffers? A once-happy marriage.

I promise you this, when you don't make time for yourself outside of your children, things will fall apart. I've been there. I know you may feel like your entire identity is being a mom, but don't lose sight of what made you YOU before kids came into existence.

Make time to connect with friends (sans kids), do a hobby that lights you up, start that business, go on dates with your partner, put the kids to bed early, make time for your fitness, get a babysitter. Whatever it is that fulfills you and gives you purpose outside of motherhood, DO IT. And be unapologetic about it. When you are at your best, you are able to give your best. And THIS is what is going to translate into a strong mom game.

Always remember, you can't pour from an empty cup.

2. Comparison truly is the thief of joy... or at least some sleepless nights.

Have you ever caught yourself observing another child and thinking, "What's wrong with my kid?" Okay, that sounds harsh, but WE ALL DO IT!

It's okay to compare, but reading too much into these comparisons or stressing over it will do nothing but rob you of a good night's sleep.

EVERYONE is different. Every child is unique and will develop at their own perfect rate. Every child also comes with their own quirks and perfect imperfections. Let them.

I had numerous sleepless nights with my first child, worried sick and googling all the things. He didn't make eye contact until he was four months old and didn't start talking until two. I was a mess. And guess what? He turned out perfect!

And the battle continued with my second son, comparing his personality and all of his milestones to his bigger brother, feeling stressed or worried if he didn't quite add up. One was running by eight months, one didn't take his first steps until 13 months.

No two kids will ever be the same. Those milestone charts? Take them with a grain of salt. Embrace and cherish every unique and amazing inch of your baby and resist the urge to compare. And if you truly have a concern, talk to your medical doctor, NOT Dr. Google. Your well-being will thank me.

3. "Super Mom" is not a thing.

You know that mom that you see at the grocery store who's in amazing shape, beautifully put together, has a cart full of organic produce waiting to be made into the perfect dinner, and two well-behaved kids walking quietly beside her (both of which are in sports uniforms because you KNOW this mom takes her kids to organized sports on the regular)? Everything about her screams "Super Mom." But spoiler alert, this mom gets ALL the help and is on the struggle bus right next to us. She is a hot mess and hides it well.

Being a mom makes you insanely badass but trying to please everyone and doing it on your own will only burn you out. I learned this the hard way. I was convinced that asking for help meant that I was incapable of being a mom, and if I didn't have the house clean and food on the table, it meant I was a shitty wife. I even went as far as saying "It's okay, I'm fine," whenever a family member or friend would reach out to offer assistance. Meanwhile, I was dying inside, and help was all I really wanted. I suffered from postpartum depression with both kids, and I think I exacerbated my condition by feeling as if I had to be Super Mom. It truly does take a village to raise a baby, so lean hard on your support system.

And if you don't want to be a Pinterest mom, then don't! Erase all guilt. Your kids need a happy mom, not a stressed out and overwhelmed one.

Ask for help OFTEN, accept help whenever it is offered, delegate duties, don't feel guilty about having a messy house or taking time for yourself, and say NO when you really don't want to do something. Being a mom is not a solo mission.

4. Embrace the mess.

Let's face it, kids are MESSY. My boys leave a trail of destruction everywhere they go. Between diaper blowouts, sticky hands, spilled Cheerios, and stained clothes, I have never done so much laundry or cleaning in my life. And this used to stress me out HUGE. It has taken me three years to finally accept the fact that "mess" is every child's middle name, and no matter how much I try to keep my kids away from the mud puddle, or out of the drawers, they still find a way to creep in and make the biggest of messes.

So calm down, Momma, and laugh it off. Better yet, join in on the fun. Jump in the mud, turn the house into a fort, dump out the toy buckets, fill a cupboard with stuff for the kids to destroy, bust out the paints, eat with your hands. It will all be okay. Laundry, housework, and dishes will pile up no matter what, so why not change your mindset toward the mess and learn to enjoy it?

The best part about allowing your kids to create a mess is that you can teach them how to clean it up (which can also be a fun game in itself)! And seriously, a spotless house is overrated anyway... are you even having fun?

5. It's okay to let your child cry.

Some people may not agree with me on this one, but from my own experience, letting my kids cry (for a short period of time of course) has been a game-changer.

Motherly instincts will kick in the second you hear your baby cry. You will want to do anything in your power to stop the crying and make your baby feel good again. Which is great! But sometimes, allowing your child to cry can be the best thing for both of you.

As a new, exhausted and overwhelmed mom with a screaming baby who won't settle, taking a step away for a couple of minutes to breathe and reset (with baby in the crib), can be the difference between a mom who snaps, and a mom who is calm and collected.

Fast forward a year or two to a screaming toddler who didn't get his way ... allowing him the space to cry it out on his own before coddling him will help him figure out his emotions and learn what behaviour is acceptable or not.

And dare I mention sleep training? Every mom's dreaded two words, because it inevitably means a whole bucketload of tears (possibly from both of you), unless you were blessed with a unicorn baby who sleeps like a dream. It has got to be one of my biggest love-hate relationships to date, but with added emphasis on LOVE. I bit the bullet early with my first child and ended up with a 4-month-old baby who slept 12-hour stretches. Denial kicked in with my second son, and I didn't fully sleep train until just last week, at 15 months of age. The tears were hard, but the payoff was huge. This momma is finally sleeping through the night!

Of course, use your motherly judgment here. If you feel your babe is in pain or truly needs you at that moment, be there. But always keep in mind that a few minutes of crying isn't going to ruin your child. Kids learn to self-soothe and better manage their emotions when they are given a bit of space to do so. And always consider your own well-being as well, because YOU matter too, Momma.

   Motherhood is a shitshow, but the most glorious and fulfilling one of all. It will never be perfect and your journey will never be the same as someone else's. Do what's best for you and your baby and enjoy this crazy ride.

Key Takeaway

Reflect on this author's work and write down one key idea, concept, or theme that you can take with you in your own life! If something really hit home, connect with the author and get social!

....
....
....
....
....
....
....
....
....
....
....
....
....
....
....
....
....
....
....

#5lessons #leadherpublishing

Chapter 18
Katie Urbanik

Find Katie: @katieurbanik

Growing up I had the idea that
I'd finish school,
become a teacher,
get married and
have x-number of kids
(probably two or three),
and everything after that would continue onward.
It was a tidy little checklist —
reasonable and straightforward.
I've always loved a good list.
I didn't think about it too much as
I finished school (check!)
and became a teacher (check!).

Years went by,
as years tend to do,
and I hadn't made any further progress toward
the next item on my list.
For a long time, I thought that I could wait it out.
The list had been made and I'd follow it accordingly.
If I happened to never make it to my final item,
well that was probably just the way it was supposed to go.
I started to wonder if I really wanted to be a mother anyway,
and for a while
I believed that story I told myself.
But as time carried on
I felt mad at the list and sad for myself.
And then I realized:
I am allowed to revise my list.
There is no extra time for waiting for things you know you want, and
I had waited long enough.
Instead of checking marriage off my list,
I crossed it out
and I moved on.
I waited my lifetime to become
a mother to the daughter
I was always meant to have
in the way
I was always meant to have her.

Reaching motherhood seemed impossible to me at times.
I learned a lot on the way,
but nothing could have prepared me for
the lessons that were waiting to be compiled into a new list:
Lessons Learned Through Motherhood.

Motherhood is a roller-coaster.
In the nine months it takes to go from

being pregnant to
becoming a mother,
you are standing in a long, winding line at an amusement park,
waiting for it to happen.
In the beginning of your pregnancy
you're at the back of the line filled with excitement that you made it
there.
You think you can kind of see what it looks like at the front,
but there's a long way to go before you get to it.
You chat with your friends and family as you slowly move
along,
gathering their stories and advice along the way.
You look back every once in a while and see
how far you've come and
look ahead to see how much farther there is to go.
As you get closer, you feel
anxious and excited,
and by the time you're at the front of the line
you're ready to get on with it already.
No matter how long that line felt when you were in it,
once you get on the ride it seems as though
it came in a flash.
One day you're rubbing your pregnant belly with a poetic
version of motherhood twinkling in your eyes,
and the next
you're in a wheelchair holding your baby
as the nurse pushes you down the hall in your post-epidur-
al-I-just-lost-a-lot-of-blood-and-can-barely-see-straight fog,
praying that you don't smash the baby's head against the
wall.

Feeding a baby isn't easy.
(And it turns out that feeding a toddler isn't easy either, but
that's another story.)

After my daughter was born
I left the hospital
with the idea that
she had a good latch.
Not because I had any idea what I was doing,
but because that's what I was told.
It turned out to be
a lie.
After a struggle,
the decision to bottle-feed came with
disappointment and relief at the same time.
Bottle-feeding turned feeding from
a stressful, tear-provoking experience into
the love fest that I had always expected it to be.
I had never heard anyone say much about it before so
I assumed
that this would continue until we moved on to solids.
By the time my daughter was seven months old,
it wasn't so lovely.
She was distracted and
I was frustrated and stressed out
before and during
every feeding.
I remember standing in front of the window
at the entrance of our house
so that she could
see the Christmas lights outside,
hopefully preoccupied by the twinkle of colours.
I had one foot up on the windowsill,
the other foot on the floor.
I was
balancing my daughter on the knee of my raised leg
facing her outwards towards the window.
I was

holding her with one arm and
holding the bottle in the hand of the other arm
while wondering,
what exactly is happening here?
This wasn't a love fest.
I was like a flamingo balancing a twenty-two pound baby on its knee.
But if she took her bottle,
I was a victorious flamingo
and that was a win I was willing to accept!

I am the world's most unapologetic hypocrite.
Everything I said I would never do,
I've done and then some.
"My baby isn't going to have a sound machine."
Cue God's laughter.
Insert: sound machine, fan, nightlight (with lights and music) and essential oil diffuser.
"My child isn't going to watch TV while she eats."
Insert: The Wiggles, Peppa Pig, Sesame Street, whatever-her-favourite-show-is-at-the-moment during breakfast, lunch, and sometimes dinner.
"My child will sit at the table for all of her meals."
Insert: me chasing her around with a forkful of macaroni and cheese while she watches *The Wiggles, Peppa Pig, Sesame Street whatever-her-favourite-show-is-at-the-moment.*
The truth is that
it's easy to be a perfect parent before you have a child.
But once I became a mother, I realized that
it's okay to do whatever it takes to make it easier.

Self-care is a practice.
Going from being on my own to having a baby meant that
the dedication of my time changed from being

one hundred percent
on myself,
to approximately
one percent
on myself and
ninety-nine percent
on my daughter.
It wasn't really
an adjustment
because there was
no adjustment period.
It happened immediately.
One day I was sauntering around my house with
nothing but time,
and the next I was spending
every waking moment
(which was every moment of the day because I was no longer
sleeping)
thinking about,
talking about,
caring about,
worrying about —
someone else.
Even when I did do something for myself,
like taking a shower,
that time wasn't spent focusing
on myself,
but on how quickly
I could get back to the baby
even if someone else was with her.
And to be honest,
that hasn't changed a lot over the years.
There still aren't any long showers because either
she's asleep and will wake up any minute

(it's an unspoken rule that when you talk or think about your child's sleep, they'll wake up),

or someone else is with her and

I should get back,

or, my favourite ...

is showering how I really want to spend my free time?

I could be sitting on the couch

(and getting up every two minutes to do a task that sitting on the couch reminded me that I needed to do).

Self-care is a practice,

as in,

it's something that I still need to practice making a priority

because while it's true that

you can't pour from an empty glass,

it's still an effort to fill the glass that will be emptied for someone else.

Self-care is another task that has to be

accomplished on a long list of things to do.

It's the thing that is flexible

and is often reordered,

usually relegated to

the bottom of the pile.

It's the one thing on the list that

is the hardest to get to,

but is

the most rewarding

once it's been

checked off.

Being a mom is painful.

It hurts

to watch your child grow up.

It hurts

to learn that
they have a life that doesn't always include you.
The worry
the fear
the hope
that you're doing this thing right is
a weight that is
invisible.
But that weight is
beautifully counteracted by
a love that is
immeasurable.
A love that makes
this ride
one that is
worth waiting for.

Key Takeaway

Reflect on this author's work and write down one key idea,
concept, or theme that you can take with you in your own life! If
something really hit home, connect with the author and get social!

....
....
....
....
....
....
....
....
....
....
....
....
....
....
....
....
....
....

Chapter 19

Elisa Prentice

Find Elisa: @elisa.prentice

We all know that little girl. The one with about a hundred dolls, always playing mommy. Many of us were her. I was her. Soon, I was able to play mommy with real babies — starting with my baby brother. At four-and-a-half, I remember being so excited from the moment that my parents told me the news, until the that moment he was born, and I was always beyond eager to help. Next trickled in all my little cousins.

As the oldest, I was so proud to help with feedings, changing diapers, playtime — you name it, I was there. I always felt like they were kind of my first babies, and I could not wait to start a family of my own. If you asked me at age 12, I would have told you that I wanted five kids. The whole damn Jackson Five. It hasn't worked out that way (yet, at least), but life has certainly brought me some beautiful blessings.

My name is Elisa. I am a 32-year-old mother to two handsome boys aged two and three-and-a-half, as well as our adopted fur baby, and I have been married to my sweetheart for over five years now. My hobbies include vacuuming (unsure why I even put it down most days), trying to get children's songs out of my head, and drinking iced coffee in between potty and snack runs. I come from a big, loud Greek family that has never shown a shortage of love, even when times are hard. My days go from sons-up, until many hours after sons-down[2]. I am perpetually tired, often under-caffeinated, and a chronic overthinker (I'm working on it, promise!). There is never a dull moment in our lives, but I choose to see the beauty in all the chaos and am learning every day. These are five of the most important things I have learned in my journey through motherhood so far.

1. You will have a good cry at least once in your life, convinced that you are a "Bad Mom."

You will weep uncontrollably at the thought that you are screwing up their lives, positive that they will end up on the wrong path and that it will all be your fault. As someone who has already done this (way) more than once in my children's short lives, let me be the first to tell you that you are not. I won't lie and say that there is no such thing as a bad mom, because we all know there definitely is, but is that you? Is that me? I highly doubt it.

Just know this — it is totally normal to feel like you aren't doing your best. Mom guilt is the realest thing ever. You will spend many of your days with one or more children hanging off your leg, or in your arms, or just plain old all up in your grill. You will crave your own space, some quiet, and some sleep. A time when you are not summoned the very second that you sit down. I am so fortunate to have an extra set of arms whenever I need them. Between my husband and our families, I have such an amazing support system. With that being said, once I finally do get a minute or an hour to myself, I automatically feel so guilty, and more often than not will cry with the thought that I am a horrible mother for needing some space. So many thoughts fill my head:

"Are they okay?"

"Did they eat?"

"Do they miss me?"

I know they're fine. I know they're fed and taken care of. I know they miss me, too, but I still feel awful. When these feelings hit you (and trust me, they will), just remember — in order for you to be the best mom you can be, you have to take care of YOU, too.

I struggle with this, big time. You are not a bad mom for wanting space. You are a great mom for wanting to be mentally healthy for your family (and most importantly, for yourself). Be kind to yourself, you are only human. When your babies lay their heads to rest at the end of a long day, they still think that you are the best mom in the world. Does anything else matter?

2. You are here to be their parent, not their best friend.

Does that suck sometimes? Totally. Just remember, they need your guidance. It's so amazing to have a little human you created who enjoys the same things that you do. It's crazy how quickly the time will pass and before you know it, they will be their own person, one you will spend so much time with and develop an incredibl friendship with. That is all good and well, but what happens when they need some discipline? They will still need to respect you as a parent and not just look at you like their best friend that is just betraying them by saying things they don't want to hear.

I don't enjoy giving those hard talks, or getting upset with my kids, but I know it must happen sometimes. I hate being looked at like the mean parent, and I so badly want to give in when I lay down a consequence like loss of screen time privileges, but then I really consider it — these kids need me, just like yours need you. We are their first teachers in life, and we must teach them well, even life's hard lessons. You will thank yourself for it later, as will they (much, much later) — or so I keep telling myself.

The last thing this world needs, in my humble opinion, is another entitled jerk walking around like the world owes them something. Please, let's stop raising them to be like that. Let's continue to raise future generations to care about others, to be polite and courteous, to genuinely give a fuck about others, to take accountability for their actions, and to give a shit about the world we live in.

Let's show our children that we can't always have what we want; life won't always go our way; and we are no better than anyone else, regardless of race, religion, gender, or sexual orientation. It starts with us. I will gladly be the bad cop when I have to be in order not to raise an asshole.

Let's all do our part.

3. They are always Listening.

Even when you don't think so, I promise that they are. This is not just a nice way of saying that they will find a way to repeat every swear word you say in front of them at the worst possible time (and good luck trying not to laugh because that shit is funny, but so, so wrong), but a reminder to carefully select the words that you use when speaking to — and in front of — them. Be aware of the good and the bad. They will always remember the things that you said, the way that you encouraged them, and the comfort that they felt because of your arms — and what came out of your mouth.

It has always been one of my goals as a parent to lead by example. I may not know how to handle every single situation, and I may not know what to say to make them feel better, or how to heal a broken heart. I may not always know the right things to say, but my heart is always in the right place. I like to make a point to admit when I'm wrong to my kids, as long as the circumstances are appropriate, and they can understand the situation. Why, you ask? I figure the answer is two-fold. On one hand, if they see me mess up and admit it, they will realize that we all fuck up sometimes, and that's just fine, we're human. On the other hand, I'm hoping that it will work both ways, and if/when they make a mistake in the future, they will feel safe coming to me with it. No matter how bad they've been on any given day, I make sure that I always tell them that I love them and I'm proud of them, because those are the words that I want them to remember — that's the Mom I want them to remember when they talk about me to their grandkids.

I feel this way mostly because when I look back on my childhood, these are the things I remember: the love, the encouragement, and the pride that my parents showed. Bottom line is, don't underestimate the ears on your little ones, even when you think they're busy. Think of them like a little sponge and fill that sponge with positivity and love as much as you can because even when a sponge gets wrung out a little bit, there will always be something left inside.

4. Time will slip through your hands.

You've heard it a million times: "They grow too fast!" I have never heard anything so true in my life. It just doesn't hit you until you actually have kids and you go from hospital to kindergarten orientation in what feels like no time flat. The days and nights are long; some are long as fuck and you start the day by counting down until bedtime — but the years are short. My advice to you is to make them count but know that it's okay to need your own space, to wish for bedtime, and to ask for help. We can only relish the moment so much.

There's not much I can say that will make you treasure every dirty diaper you change, every load of laundry, every sleepless night, but take some time to remember them when they are little. I love writing in my kid's baby books, and every time I do, I flip to the beginning and look at their ultrasound pictures. I read the words I wrote to them when they were just plum-sized in my belly, and I cry every time.

If you knew me, you'd know how emotional I am, but there's something about my kids that sets it off even more than anything else. I clearly remember the days I found out that I was pregnant with each of them, and it feels like just yesterday and a lifetime ago. Every day, they wake up a little older and a little wiser, and I hate to say it but a little more independent than the last. Remember their sweet little giggle, their drooly smiles, the way they smell.

One day, we will pick our babies up for the last time and not even know it. I'm not going to lie and say that the very thought doesn't tear me up inside. So, no matter how busy I am, I always get on the floor and play with them. Dishes can wait. I take a million pictures and videos of them, never wanting to forget a smile or a silly dance. No matter what time of day or night, I will always cuddle. Who needs sleep anyway? You will never regret the time spent with your children. I know I won't.

5. You are the only one who knows what works best for your children.

From the moment you get pregnant, the advice begins. You will have nearly every mother and grandmother you come across giving you tips on what worked for them (or their sister, best friend, second cousin twice removed) during pregnancy, birth, and parenthood. I will fully acknowledge that most of them do not have ill intentions and that giving mothers and mothers-to-be advice is just what people do. I get that. What I want you to know, though, is that not all of those things will work for you and your family. Maybe all of them will, maybe none of them will, and that's okay! At the end of the day, you are the only one that will be able to deem what is best for you and your family. You are the centre of it all, Mama, and you will be the only one who knows what works.

It's crazy to think that we all enter motherhood pretty much blind, and although some days may feel like we are feeling our way around in the dark, we figure it out pretty quickly. Motherly intuition is incredible. Moms just know. Even when they don't know, they *know* — you know? I love thinking that one day I will be looked at with the same knowledge that we look to my grandma for. Will we ever know everything? No, of course not but through years and years of trial and error, and a mix of going with the flow and overthinking the shit out of everything, we will know what worked for us. My advice to you is don't sweat it when you don't fit into the same box as your cousin's best friend's sister, or whatever the case may be. You've got this.

Among the plethora of lessons, both good and bad, that I continue to learn every day (and sometimes more than once a day), motherhood has truly made me realize how different everyone's journey to it — and through it — can be, and yet how similar they all are at the same time. Let's continue to support each other in our journeys. Let's lift women up.

We are all in this together!

Key Takeaway

Reflect on this author's work and write down one key idea, concept, or theme that you can take with you in your own life! If something really hit home, connect with the author and get social!

....
....
....
....
....
....
....
....
....
....
....
....
....
....
....
....
....

#5lessons #leadherpublishing

Chapter 20

Laura Lorentz

Author Photo: Cathy Fyfe
Find Laura: @laura.e.lorentz

When I was in high school, I had my next ten to fifteen years planned out: go to university, get a good job, climb the corporate ladder, get married before 30, and have kids in my early 30s. I'm a planner by nature, so it's no surprise that I graduated from university, moved to downtown Toronto, made several ladder-climbing career moves, and got married, all by 2 years old. Things were going exactly as planned. In fact, I was ahead of my schedule.

I loved everything about living in Toronto: the hustle, the bustle, the restaurants, my friends, and most importantly, my career. As mentioned, I climbed the corporate ladder relatively quickly. I was 26 years old and managing relationships with my company's largest clients. I was responsible for setting strategic growth plans and negotiating operating contracts with men often twice my age.

I traveled across the country and attended strategic planning sessions in beautiful destinations like Napa Valley. I reported to a Senior Vice President who supported me and my desire to hold a senior leadership position in the near future. I had everything I wanted in my career.

That's when I felt "the pull," or the biological clock as some may call it. At 27 years old, I felt a strong desire to be a mom. However, when I thought about the life I wanted to have raising my kids, it wasn't in downtown Toronto. I wanted to be close to family. I wanted my kids to experience the childhood that I had growing up in Kitchener, Ontario.

That's when my husband and I made the decision to move back to our hometown.

I was excited for the next chapter in my life. I had accomplished so much and was ready to take on this new challenge. However, looking back, I wasn't prepared for the events that unfolded next.

Over the next two years, I became lost in my career, and I went through a very emotionally challenging miscarriage. I was no longer the person I was in Toronto and I went through a major grieving process. But when I became pregnant with my daughter, Ellery, my world began to change. Light was brought back into my life, and in many ways, I look at it as a rebirth.

My name is Laura Lorentz. I am a Corporate Queen, Side Hustling Entrepreneur, Craft Beer Enthusiast, mama to my 1-year-old daughter, Ellery, a Goldendoodle named Floyd, and soon-to-be mama to baby #2 in January 2021.

Now that you know a bit more about me, here are my 5 lessons learned through motherhood.

1. Share your story because it may help someone who needs to hear it.

When I went through my miscarriage, I felt many emotions including grief, shame, guilt, and anger. At 12 weeks pregnant, my husband and I shared with all of our friends and family that we were pregnant. I hadn't been for my first-trimester scan yet, but I felt great and didn't have any complications. At 13 weeks, however, my world came crashing down when the technician didn't detect a heartbeat during the ultrasound. I felt grief for the loss of our baby. I felt shame because I had just shared our news and now I'd have to tell everyone about our loss. I felt guilt because I wondered if I did something wrong to cause it. And, I felt anger that I didn't know sooner since the technician estimated that the baby had passed at about seven weeks. I had a missed miscarriage, which meant that I had no signs of loss other than no heartbeat detected through an ultrasound.

Through this situation, many women who I knew shared their stories of pregnancy loss with me. Their stories comforted me. They made me feel like I wasn't alone, and they also gave me hope because many of these women went on to have very healthy pregnancies afterward. I appreciated the women who shared their stories with me, and I now know how important it is to share my story. Not only can it help other women get through a difficult time and normalize the occurrence of pregnancy loss, I found it helped me work through my own emotions.

Similar to pregnancy experiences, I have come to realize the importance of sharing birth stories. About seven months after my daughter was born, I was asked to share my birth story on a podcast (Love Your Cells[3] podcast by Sue Rhue). I was honored to be a part of it, as I remember how clueless I was going into my delivery and how I wished someone had told me all of the normal things that happen that I

[3]https://directory.libsyn.com/shows/view/id/loveyourcellspodcast

wasn't aware of. There were so many things that I was self-conscious about, and I remember thinking, "Oh gosh, my husband will never look at me the same way again after this experience." From my humiliating water-breaking experience to my husband seeing my hemorrhoids during delivery, to him having to help "milk me" to initiate breast milk production, it all seemed so embarrassing at the time. We have come to laugh about it now and I think he loves me more because of it, but there was a point when I was worried that he would never love me again.

Overall, I am so grateful to be a part of this book and sharing my story. I hope it inspires you, comforts you, and brings light to all of the normal things that happen during pregnancy, birth, and beyond. You've got this!

2. You can't control everything.

After our miscarriage in 2018, it took us about seven months to get pregnant again. Every month that passed with a negative pregnancy test was a constant reminder of our loss. My life became consumed with ovulation tests, googling how to increase my likelihood of getting pregnant, and counting down the days until I could take the next pregnancy test. It wasn't the exciting experience that I thought it would be, and honestly, it felt like a job that I had to do. I knew I was fortunate enough to get pregnant but waiting and not being able to control the circumstances took a toll on my mental health, focus at work, and relationships with those dear to me. Looking back, I now see it as a lesson and the initial introduction into motherhood. When you become a mom, you quickly learn that there are very few situations you can control; from midnight wakeups, to teething, to growth spurts, to temper tantrums, the list is endless. At the end of the day, our role as parents is not to control our kids' lives, rather it is to support them and guide them. They make their own choices and we are there to guide them along the way.

3. Motherhood is a constant duality.

From the moment that you find out you are pregnant, the duality begins. You are so excited about this new bundle of joy coming into your life, but at the same time, there is a feeling of fear. You want to be positive and optimistic, but you are also aware of the very real scenarios where things could go wrong. Once your child is born, you are overjoyed that you are holding this precious creation, but you are tired as hell and your body aches. When your baby has been crying for three hours straight at 2:00 a.m., you are frustrated beyond belief, but oddly grateful that you are in this situation. You may love being home with your baby, but miss work at the same time. You may want to cuddle your baby, but also scream. You may hate the way your body looks, but love and respect it for all that it can do. These dualities never go away and I have learned to embrace them. They are both a part of me. I've also learned that it is okay to acknowledge when things get overwhelming. We are only human, so being compassionate with ourselves is necessary.

4. Be who you want your kids to be.

I believe with all of my heart that this is fundamental to raising awesome human beings. However, I'll be honest, this lesson was a tough one for me because it required me to take a good hard look at my life and how I was showing up day to day. I thought of all the things that I wanted to teach my daughter: you can be anything you want to be, love yourself, be authentic, don't be afraid, chase your dreams, be grateful, enjoy the simple things in life, and so much more. When I thought of all these things, I realized that I wasn't living half of them.

Over the last year and a bit, I have consciously been focusing on improving my mindset and myself. I have invested in myself in so many ways that I never would have before. I started a business, set aside alone time, took time to appreciate what I have, saw my therapist, and hired a coach. I've learned that if I don't focus on myself and my own passions, I'm not able to show up and be the role model I want to be for my kids. At the end of the day, our kids model our behaviours, not our words.

5. Motherhood is a rebirth.

Just as your child is birthed into this world, a new you is birthed into this world as well. Not only are there physical changes to your body, but there are also emotional changes. There are studies that show how a woman's brain changes after she gives birth. There is a shift in the amount of grey matter in various parts of the brain, so when you feel different, you actually *are* different. It's completely normal for your values, beliefs, or ambitions to change.

This is why it is a very common time for women to question key parts of their lives like their career paths, relationships, hobbies, etc. For me, I was tired of doing things because it was the "right thing to do," or it was the next step in my plan. It was time to focus on what makes me happy. My maternity leave allowed me time away from my everyday life to assess what was important and I discovered that it was family, and taking time to actually enjoy life. During my mat leave, I spent lots of time watching my daughter grow, learn, and explore. My husband and I went golfing, we made really delicious food, and spent lots of time at our family cottages. I made less money than I have since I was 21 years old, but it honestly didn't matter.

I realize now that my overachiever mentality deprived me from the things that I craved in life the most — joy, happiness, and gratitude.

With that said, I still enjoy my work and consider myself ambitious, however I am much more focused on doing what I enjoy, rather than what is good for my resume or what other people expect of me. I've really slowed down, but I am starting to feel really comfortable where I am (for the first time in my life).

Key Takeaway

Reflect on this author's work and write down one key idea, concept, or theme that you can take with you in your own life! If something really hit home, connect with the author and get social!

....

....

....

....

....

....

....

....

....

....

....

....

....

....

....

....

....

....

Chapter 21
Marijke Visser

Find Marijke: @wildlycapableyou

Hey Mamas! I am *Marijke Visser*. I am a mother, a fitness mentor, a mental health advocate, and I have been working with children for over 10 years. I recently became a host for my very own podcast called *Mental Health & Motherhood With Marijke*[*]. I love helping and encouraging women to take care of their own mental health needs while raising their children confidently, with a positive perspective.

When I became a mom, I was in the middle of my college studies and thought about giving my daughter up for adoption. I was not "ready" to be a mother. I was unmarried, hadn't finished school and this did not align with my perception of how life went. I am so thankful that I had the support around me to succeed. It was messy and it was hard but I learned that I can persevere through challenges, and that I would never change my decision to keep my daughter.

When I first became a mother, I thought there was a specific way that I had to parent and I made every choice based on what I thought other moms would do. I was lost in the darkness of mental illness and had no idea that I had the ability to fight back with the right resources and support.

At the beginning of 2019, I decided that I was done living a life controlled by fear, comparison, depression, and anxiety. I wanted more for my family, and for myself.

In February 2019, I moved across the country. This was a big change that I needed to start helping myself move beyond fear and anxiety.

For the last year-and-a-half, I have been able to make big steps toward being the mother and person I have always wanted to be, including taking care of my own mental health by taking time for myself; launching a podcast, and writing this chapter. These were all things that I thought I could never do because it was not "motherly" to have your own goals and aspirations outside of motherhood.

No matter what stage of motherhood you are in, *please, please, please* make time for yourself, and stop comparing your journey to everyone else's! Choose to parent the way that feels good for you and works for your family. You know your child(ren) best, so you know what is best for them!

Although I wholeheartedly believe that you know what is best for your child, I think that every mama can use a few helpful tips, from one mama to another, to improve her own motherhood journey. These are five things that I've learned on my journey so far; but make no mistake, I will continue to learn and grow!

1. You do NOT have to go this alone!

This lesson is by far the most important lesson I have learned! You do NOT have to go this alone. I thought for so long that I could not admit to anyone else that I was struggling and did not ask for help for a long time. I thought that asking for help was a sign of weakness. I was completely wrong!

You may feel like you need to be this "strong" mother who goes through her challenges all alone. The thing is, asking for help is a sign of strength, a sign that you understand that the challenges you are facing are too big for you, for any one person, to handle alone. Asking for help is the single most important thing that you can do to help yourself, and your family.

When I started reaching out to other people and sharing my struggles, it became the support that I needed to handle my challenges. Find your people, whoever and wherever they may be — whether they are in the same season, different season, or have been in a similar season of life before you. Each person you have is important and valuable because they all have some treasure to share and a different way to support you.

It is important to surround yourself with people who will support you through your struggles — through the good and the bad times. They will share what they have learned and the things they are continuing to learn.

Take time to celebrate your wins with your people, no matter how small. Celebrate each other instead of comparing yourselves to one another. If they have overcome something that you are currently struggling with, they are PROOF that it is possible to overcome it. Maybe you are like the old me and think asking for help makes you look weak, incapable, and unworthy of being a mama.

IT DOES NOT!

"It takes a village to raise a child." Go find your village to support your own development both as a mother and as a person! You need other people to offer advice, love, and support during your best moments and also during the worst moments. You need them and they need you!

2. Love extends BEYOND blood!

This was a lesson that my mother taught me as I was growing up. She always extended warm arms to everyone she met, showed compassion, non-judgment, and really, just pure love. I never fully understood this lesson until a few months into my pregnancy.

I was a few months pregnant when I met my oldest, non-biological, daughter. In our house there have never been labels like stepsister, stepmother or stepfather; it is just family.

Family can be complicated and messy but you do NOT have to be blood-related to love children the same way that a mother would love them. You can form a connection that is composed so deeply that no one can tear it apart. I am honoured and blessed to have two 'bonus' daughters, and I raise them the same as I do my biological daughter.

To develop a pure, real connection, and a mother-child relationship full of love, it is going to be HARD. You will have to work a little harder to form the connection, BUT let me tell you this. IT IS 100% achievable to form a motherly bond with children who are not blood-related to you and it is 100% worth the fight to develop that relationship.

Maybe you're dating and just met a man who has children, or you cannot have any biological children of your own, or you have children of your own and are considering adoption to continue to grow your family. Whatever the situation, know that pure, real love extends beyond blood.

3. Your feelings are VALID!

Why do we as mothers often make ourselves feel bad for our feelings or minimize the feelings that we have? "I don't have it that bad compared to Sally Sue, so I should not feel like this." Let me tell you, here and now, that your feelings are just as valid as another mother's feelings.

We all experience and feel things differently and that's okay. It's actually totally and completely normal. When we start to minimize our feelings, they just bottle up or we start this nasty shame cycle with ourselves. In psychology, this is called minimization, defined as inappropriately shrinking something to make it seem less important Sound familiar to what you do with your feelings?

Instead, ACCEPT your feelings, sit with them for a while, then let them out, and when you are able to process them and move forward, do something to take care of yourself. Sometimes those feelings may be short, and other times they may last a little longer.

You are human, you will have a multitude of feelings, especially during motherhood. There may be times where you feel like you hate being a mother, feel angry at the way your life is, feel exhausted, and feel like you just want to quit. That's okay! There will also be times when you feel blessed and honoured to be a mother, feel so much joy, and are excited about what your life looks like. It all balances out!

So take time today to validate your feelings, because no matter what the situation is and what your feelings about it are, all the feelings and emotions you are feeling are valid, and they are true to who you are. Make space for your emotions and feelings and expect that they will be all over the place throughout your motherhood journey

4. Grow WITH your children!

When I became a mom, I thought and felt that 100% of my time and energy had to go toward my children. I was always exhausted and burned out, but I just thought that was the way it was supposed to be. When I started taking time for myself in the morning while the rest of the house was sleeping, I started to enjoy my days more. Without even realizing it, by taking this time every day for myself I started growing. My daughter is a witness to this change.

During this quiet "me" time, I focus on filling up my cup so that whatever is thrown my way during the day, I can stay calm and handle it more easily. When we begin to put ourselves first, we no longer feel as burned out, exhausted, irritable, or tense. It is when we put ourselves last that our cup is constantly empty.

When you start making time for yourself, for *your* mental growth and focus on *your* goals and aspirations, you will be able to find so much more joy in motherhood.

Growth doesn't stop as soon as you become a mother. Instead, as a mother, you have this incredible opportunity to not only watch your children grow, but to also have them watch you continually grow as well.

Share how you're growing and challenging yourself with your family, so they can watch how you handle success, stress, mistakes, failure, and most importantly, how you grow. This teaches them valuable life skills about how to handle challenges and it also teaches them to make time for themselves to make sure their cup is filled before serving and supporting others.

5. Give yourself GRACE upon GRACE!

The first four years of my motherhood journey I filled my head with constant shame and guilt that I was not doing it right or that I was not a good enough mother for my daughter.

Give yourself grace! Grace for the unexpected life you live. Grace for the bumps along the way. Grace because motherhood is HARD work! We are human and we all make mistakes. It does not serve you or your family to shame yourself or hold shame inside of you and let it boil up or tear you down. Talk to yourself and support yourself as you would your best friend or your child.

A bad day does not make you a bad mother, or a bad person! Motherhood is full of a number of unexpected curve balls that we're all constantly trying to juggle (what can sometimes feel like a million balls!) at once. Once in a while, and maybe even every day for a while, a few of those balls are going to fall and drop off, and you just have to accept it. In those moments, what you need to do is look at all the balls that you kept up in the air! Look at all the balls that you've been able to juggle longer, higher, and better than you ever expected, and celebrate all of your wins — big or small!

There are going to be hard days and hard moments when you do not want to keep pushing or feel like you cannot keep going. The thing is, you will persevere because you have done A LOT of hard things before. There have been many times in your life when you thought you could not do something because it was too hard, but you got through it and you grew because of it.

Take a moment now to give yourself compassion and grace. All mothers are struggling in their own way, yet we are all still learning and growing. We grow even stronger when we support each other and build a foundation of pure love — both for our families and for ourselves.

Now, take a moment every day to remind yourself:

You are a WARRIOR!
You have more STRENGTH and RESILIENCE than you know!
You have the POWER and DURABILITY inside of yourself!
You are wildly CAPABLE!
You are WORTHY!

Key Takeaway

Reflect on this author's work and write down one key idea, concept, or theme that you can take with you in your own life! If something really hit home, connect with the author and get social!

....
....
....
....
....
....
....
....
....
....
....
....
....
....
....
....

Chapter 22
Darci Prince

Author Photo: Bill Martindale
Find Darci: @darciiprince

I still don't consider myself to be a mom. I mean, I still call my mom for things, so how can I actually be someone's mom? I only baked my first batch of homemade cookies two days ago; I didn't even know how to properly make corn-on-the-cob until last year; I still don't know how to iron properly or change a tire on my car, and yet I'm somehow responsible for keeping a tiny human alive. It blows my mind how we're required to take part in so much training to work a job or drive a car, and yet we birth a human being and a few days later — or sometimes the same day — we're allowed to just walk out of the hospital with it; what in the actual hell is that about? Where's the training manual for that?

I'm Darci Prince and I'm responsible for keeping a 20-month old little boy alive on the daily. His name is Grayson and he is the brightest spot in my life — but he has also been one of the sources of some dark spots. I'm going to be straight up here — because I promised myself that I would be when I took on this project — I had a rough pregnancy, a tough recovery after Grayson made his arrival, and I struggled with postpartum depression on my maternity leave.

Being a mom was a massive adjustment for me because I had never felt "baby fever" and therefore there was no void that I felt needed to be filled by this little being. Please understand, I LOVE MY LITTLE HUMAN! He is so smart, adorable, and absolutely hilarious; he makes me laugh every single day. But hot damn, it has been a tough road. And even though everyone says, "It'll get easier," well, I'm still waiting.

I've always been afraid to say these things to those who don't have kids yet, are soon-to-be-moms, or are new moms because I don't want them to think it's all horrible; it's not! But it's also not all butterflies and rainbows that are commonly shown on social media. I think it's important to know that if and when you aren't glowing and madly in love with your human every second of every day, IT IS OKAY! So here it is, real and in print for all to read!

As you read through my *5 Lessons Learned Through Motherhood* (so far), you'll notice a recurring theme — I don't know what the hell I'm doing. But I don't think anyone does. We all just have to figure out what works for us and roll with it. So, to any new moms, seasoned moms, or soon-to-be moms, YOU'RE A ROCKSTAR AND YOU WILL SURVIVE!

1. There's no right way to do it.

Whether the stick or the doctor told you, you're pregnant — woohoo! Now what? Call the friends and family, and head to the bookstore to start studying. But be warned, once you make it even slightly known that you've asked someone for advice, it'll start coming in tidal waves, whether you want it or not!

Buckle up, here comes the onslaught of information of how-to's, and "here's-what-I-did" stories. The books, the family members, the social media platforms, the mommy-bloggers, everyone has done it their own way. Everyone will tell you how to parent, and how it "should" be done. Well, guess what? What worked for them, may not work for you! Or, it worked great for their first, but didn't work at all for their second!

Ever wonder why there are so many books, blogs, and opinions? It's because **there is no perfect formula!** None of us know what we're doing. Each mom knows what miraculously kept their humans alive, but that's about it. Here's the secret formula: keep them breathing, fed, and changed, then you're doing it the right way!

2. Formula feeding = freedom (for me)

Due to my ongoing struggle with mental health, I knew that it would be disastrous for me, the baby, and our family if I were the only one who could keep our baby fed. I had no interest in discussing nursing from day one and was adamant about this throughout my entire pregnancy. I explained this to people who seemed genuinely interested in our firm decision, but eventually, I stopped feeling the need to justify it.

But let me tell you, I took a lot of crap from people about this! I was accused of withholding the best possible nutrients from my baby, was told that formula would make sense only if breastfeeding didn't work, was informed that breastfeeding is what you're "supposed" to do, and was frequently asked why we were going to waste money on "the stuff from the store" when I could feed our baby for free. So, where's the freedom? Well ...

Thanks to formula feeding, my husband and I were able to send our son for his first sleepover at two weeks old! We never went for more than one month without a full night's sleep and a night to ourselves. *Thank you, formula.*

When we had visitors, they'd get non-stop cuddles for hours and I could read or go to the store and have some me time, without having to take the baby back so that he could eat. *Thank you, formula.*

When our son woke up in the middle of the night, I didn't have to do every feed! I could roll over and (try to) go back to sleep. My husband was able to do some of the feedings and spent so much one-on-one time with our son because he could cuddle while feeding him. Thank you, formula.

Was it an added expense? Yes.

Was the freedom that the formula gave us worth it? AB-SO-FREAK-ING-LOUTELY!

3. It takes an army, so gather up your troops.

When your baby is born and they're still fresh, new, and exciting, you get a ton of messages saying some version of "let me know if you need anything." Unfortunately, a lot of those end up being empty offers.

The people you can count on are the people who your child will grow up TRULY knowing. Your people are the ones who call when they're at the grocery store and say, "I'm at the store, what do you need?" They're the ones who say, "I'm on my way over, you're going to have a shower and a nap." They're the ones who come over when you call them bawling at all hours when the baby will not stop crying.

It doesn't take a village — it takes an army. And don't be surprised if the people who make up that army might not be who you thought they would be when you used to imagine your adult life. But that army is here now, so welcome them with open arms, and hand over that baby! Go get some sleep!

4. There's another type of solo-parenting.

The traditional definition of a solo-parent: someone who is parenting on their own while their partner is away for extended periods of time, often due to circumstances such as deployment.

My husband works in the trades. This means that while scheduled for an 8-hour day, he is actually gone from our home for 12+ hours on a daily basis.

Since the baby wakes up after my husband leaves for work and is back in bed before he gets home, 90% the time I'm the only one who is able to take care of the tiny human. So even though I am happily married in a two-income household, a lot of the time I am doing this alone. I figure out daycare around my work schedule, I take care of the house and make dinners, I do bath time, and bedtime routine. It is mostly on me; I'm a working mom and a solo-parent.

Please understand that this is equally as hard for my husband. After working a long day of physical labour, he gets home from work to a wife who is emotionally drained, and sometimes a sobbing pile of a human being on the floor. He's missed yet another day of our baby's life. He is defeated. I am defeated. It is hard on everyone. Nothing about this is easy, but we're getting by.

This is a touchy subject because from the outside, we're happy, we're married, and life is good. So, to my single friends who are parenting on their own, I don't want this to appear as though I'm complaining, but I want to put it out there that this is just as hard, but it is a different type of hard.

Shout-out to Stephanie (@stephanie_obrien_) who introduced me to solo-parenting in this context.

5. Postpartum depression isn't always immediate.

After your baby is born you watch videos on SIDS and Postpartum Depression, and you expect it to be immediate. You suspect that it might happen to you because you might not bond with your baby right away. Well, with my history of mental health issues, I was DEFINITELY expecting it. But it never came. I loved my baby boy from the second I held him. I adored everything about him and never felt dread toward caring for him. The months went by and I was relieved because we had made it through. I had made it through.

Then it happened.

We were five months in when it hit me. It was the week leading up to my first Mother's Day, and I wanted nothing to do with my baby boy. I would cry and hyperventilate when he would cry or need something. I couldn't be near him. I spent my first Mother's Day barely holding my own baby because I couldn't stand to breathe the same air as him. It breaks my heart to say this, but it was our reality.

After sending our little boy for ongoing sleepovers for two weeks, numerous counseling sessions, and an adjustment of the medication that I was already on, things leveled out, and it got better. It always gets better.

I just have to remember that this is normal, and it's fucking hard, and that's okay.

It's also normal to need help. It's normal to think that it's hard. It's normal to ask for help. It's normal to send your child for as many sleepovers as you want. It's normal to do whatever you need to do to keep yourself sane. If you aren't taking care of yourself, you won't be able to take care of your little human. Be kind to yourself. It's the best thing you can do for you, your tiny human, and your family.

Key Takeaway

Reflect on this author's work and write down one key idea,

concept, or theme that you can take with you in your own life! If

something really hit home, connect with the author and get social!

....
....
....
....
....
....
....
....
....
....
....
....
....
....
....
....
....
....
....
....

Chapter 23

Ashley Zarb

Author Photo: MDD Photography
Find Ashley: @ashleyzarbinteriors | @zarnacchia

always envisioned motherhood coming naturally to me. I thought it would be much easier than it has been. That is not to say that I don't love being a mom, because I absolutely do. But my journey into motherhood did not start off quite as you would imagine.

When I found out I was pregnant with my firstborn, I was overjoyed. Having a baby is supposed to be one of life's greatest gifts. Unfortunately, at the time, I was experiencing severe issues with my mother and was surrounded by her negativity. As my pregnancy progressed and my daughter was born, my mother's behaviour worsened — her lack of control over me as I entered into a new stage of life caused more emotional abuse than ever before. My support system was weak. I felt alone.

My problems with my mother also strained my relationship with my husband. There were constant battles about how my family was treating me and us. He didn't understand that I knew no other normal. Fights, being blamed for everything that went wrong, constantly tip-toeing around my mom — I lived my life to please and gain acceptance from my mother.

I knew I wanted my daughter to grow up in a different environment but didn't know where to start. Months later, I began therapy and my path of healing. I finally started to see things for what they really were. There was a long road ahead of me — who was I, really? After years of being told who to be, I was finally discovering myself. I was creative, strong, and sensible. My feelings were valid and there were so many other people who cared for me. I no longer found the need to live my life to gain the acceptance, support and love from my mom; I was truly okay with being and living as me.

Although therapy was the hardest thing I've ever done, I can truly say that it helped me discover myself and learn how the past affected me. I now know that my history is not my legacy.

My name is Ashley. I am a full-time Coordinator, wife, mom of two, and aspiring home decorator.

Though much of what I have learned through motherhood happened in the early years of my daughter's life, the birth of my son also taught me a thing or two. My learning is only just beginning, but I am better equipped and ready for it now.

1. You will be forced to look within.

Have you ever felt irritated or triggered by something, but didn't quite understand why? Never in my wildest dreams did I think that my past would resurface. The past is the past, right? I was very wrong.

When my daughter was born, many uncertainties began to arise. Every day, I questioned my ability as a mother. I had a hard time connecting with my daughter and understanding her needs. In many ways, I struggled. I was not only dealing with postpartum "baby blues," I lacked confidence in myself. I had no one to tell me what to do, which I was so conditioned for.

I needed to look within and understand why I doubted myself. I longed for a healthy mother-daughter relationship — something I never had. I strived to be different from my mother — more genuine, less controlling, and understanding of others. I wanted to create a safe and healthy environment for my children to grow and thrive. This caused me to overcompensate in how I treated my daughter. I never wanted her to go through what I did. I never wanted her to feel abandoned or that her feelings were not important or valid. Unresolved trauma was holding me back.

When I went to therapy, I learned that childhood trauma can fester into so many areas of your life, including your relationships with your own children. Instead of acting how you actually want, the brain's natural response is to react to circumstances or events in the way you were taught.

For me, dealing with my past helped me look at my life from a more balanced perspective. Instead of constantly trying to protect my daughter from how I felt as a child, I see her as an individual with her own needs and emotions.

Yes, the past is the past, but deeply rooted issues have a way of resurging if they are not recognized and overcome.

2. You do you.

"You should ..." — When you have a child, you will hear this phrase constantly. You will hear it more and more, and it will probably get to your head. Even if you don't ask for advice, it will be voluntarily given. I genuinely believe it's a person's way to offer help and seek connection and validation, but feedback is often expressed in the wrong way.

Every child is so deeply and inherently unique. There is no one-size-fits-all approach to parenting. So, if you find yourself trying not to nurse your baby during the night because someone told you it will turn into a bad habit — STOP!

Do what works for you, because at the end of the day, someone will still comment or pass some sort of judgement — and that's OKAY!

There are so many phases and changes in motherhood. It is a learning process for both mom and child. When I look back, the infancy phase was much easier than it felt in the moment. It was a lot of nursing, changing, and cuddles, which felt overwhelming at the time; whereas now, it is more physically and emotionally demanding. They are both full of energy and emotions they do not understand, and I'm trying to let them work through it in an accepting and healthy manner.

Take the time to learn about your son or daughter and block out the noise. Find a way to navigate through the phase in the present moment and accept it. Accepting the phase that you're in will make it so much easier to get through it as your best self.

3. Partnership is key.

This may seem like a no brainer, but my husband and I did not understand the magnitude of parenthood.

I have known my husband since childhood. After marriage, we began to plan our family. We discussed having four children (that quickly changed after two). We knew everything about each other — or so we thought — until our eldest was born. Adding another tiny human to the mix definitely changed the dynamic of our relationship.

I had no idea what I was doing and took motherhood very seriously. He, on the other hand, was more laid back about pretty much everything. Motherhood was new to me, but parenthood was new to both of us. We adjusted in different ways and realized there was no right or wrong way to approach the new changes in our lives. We quickly learned how important communication is. How to parent, how to share responsibilities, how to respect and understand each other, how to find personal time for ourselves — talking about the hard stuff is crucial and endless in a marriage. Open and respectful communication must be practiced and honed. It is difficult, but essential, for your relationship and children.

Motherhood is a crazy journey, but ultimately, you are not in it alone. Your spouse is your partner, and you need to be there for each other every step of the way.

4. Love conquers all.

You have probably heard the saying, "You need to love yourself in order to love others." While it may be cliché, loving yourself is extremely important.

In my journey, loving myself did not come easy. I actually had no idea how to care for and love myself at all, as my childhood and adolescent years were spent caring for my mother's emotions and doing anything possible to feel loved and accepted by her. I had to acknowledge this and accept my childhood experiences, let go, and relearn what healthy love looks like.

Part of loving yourself is understanding your emotions and respecting how you feel. Just as you soothe a crying baby or practice calming techniques with your children, take a step back and don't forget about you — love yourself, your emotions, and your body. Heck, just give yourself a hug once in a while.

Taking the time to reflect and journal about my feelings helped me reassess my emotions and become self-compassionate. Once I started showing myself love, I was able to care and support others so much more easily.

It is so easy to forget yourself when you're juggling work and a family, but if you practice self-love, the universe has its way of letting the other pieces fall together.

5. YOU are a good mom.

I don't know about you, but I still question myself when it comes to being "a good mom." What is a good mom, really? To some, it's spending every moment with their children, educating them, being proud of who they are, or cooking homemade meals, and being a stay-at-home parent. For others, it's teaching them respect, confidence, faith, mindfulness, and responsibility.

Whichever path you choose, YOU ARE A GOOD MOM. You are genuinely concerned about nourishing their bodies and their emotional and mental well-being, which leads to healthy self-love for their spiritual nourishment. That comes from a desire to love and want the best for your children. THAT is a "good mom."

There is no perfect mother who has it all together. Everyone has their own unique set of experiences and challenges, but striving for perfectionism is a downward spiraling slope. It can lead you to unattainable standards or unrealistic goals, resulting in hopelessness and low self-worth. When we are in this state, it's hard to be a mom, period.

So, don't strive for perfection. All you need to do is put your best self forward — that is GOOD ENOUGH and no one will love you any more or any less because of it.

Key Takeaway

Reflect on this author's work and write down one key idea, concept, or theme that you can take with you in your own life! If something really hit home, connect with the author and get social!

....
....
....
....
....
....
....
....
....
....
....
....
....
....
....
....
....
....

Chapter 24
Victoria Salerno

Find Victoria: @vivivictorious | @therestedranch

"My kid will never be like that."

Before I was a mom, I used to think that when I looked at other people's kids. How appalling to judge something I had zero experience in myself. I am by no means a parenting expert. I am learning as I go, as I think we all are. Geez, I only have a year or so under my belt as a mom. But I'll tell ya, I have learned more about myself and how I, now, choose to be, than I have in my entire life.

My name is Victoria. I'm an influencer marketing professional, a certified sleep coach, and a beauty enthusiast. I married the love of my life in 2018, and in the summer of 2019, the best thing ever happened. I became a mom to a perfect baby boy, Humphrey.

Motherhood changed me in so many incredible ways, and I have learned a lot throughout this new journey. If I must narrow it down to the top five lessons that I've learned so far, here they are:

1. Find your #Momfidence.

This one is real. Like very REE-YULL. As a first-time mom, you may feel lost and clueless with every new stage you enter into. The biggest thing that pushed me to find my mom-confidence, was breastfeeding. Let me start this by saying fed is best — period. No matter how you feed your baby, you're doing it right. I chose to breastfeed. Going into it, I kept thinking of all the backlash moms get from formula feeding. I felt so nervous that if I were to ever formula feed instead that I would be met with incredible judgment. I never once thought of the shaming that came with breastfeeding. Not ... once. Until I lived it.

Apparently in the Mother & Baby Unit of the hospital, they are supposed to teach you how to breastfeed. Being a first-time mom, I had no idea. Perhaps there was a glitch in the system somewhere, but no one came to teach me. I had a crazy instinct that too much time had passed, and I needed to feed Humphrey. So, I tried. I picked him up and did what I saw other moms do — placed him on my breast and hoped for the best. Obviously, nothing happened. I quickly asked my husband to search in our hospital bags and pass me my phone. I taught myself how to breastfeed through YouTube.

I worked really hard. I took all the supplements, drank all the teas, baked all the cookies, and felt like I was either feeding or pumping 24/7. A feeding, pumping zombie. It was exhausting. In the thick of me working tirelessly to breastfeed my son, I was met with passionate judgment. In retrospect, this probably helped expedite the discovery of my own "momfidence."

"How do you know you're producing enough?", "Breast milk is too watery!", "You're going to feed him in public?" And the looks! Oh ... the looks I would get if I fed him in public. Even ... wait for it ... at the hospital. We, unfortunately, had to go to the ER when Humphrey was small and while we were in the waiting room, he was hungry. So, I fed him. There were two young boys, perhaps early 20s, glar-

ing at me the entire time, making me feel incredibly uncomfortable. And all I could think about was how their parents likely never
taught them that breastfeeding was beautifully natural. I bet no one
shames them when their mom provides dinner for them? Potato,
po-tah-to, no?

I felt like I was struggling so much for a fight that no one wanted
me to win. Then, I found @leadherpublishing & @thelittlemilkbar on
Instagram and my confidence journey started to change. It wasn't
long after, that I started to breastfeed in public and at the dinner
table, with confidence.

Best momfidence moment: Feeding my son in a Foot Locker, on
Boxing Day, right beside people trying on shoes. WHAT'S UP?

Find your momfidence, girl! If you are struggling, take this as a sign
to pat yourself on the back, recognize all of your hard work and how
kickass of a mom you really are.

2. Mom shaming is very real. It sucks. Don't be that person.

Halsey, American singer/songwriter, recently tweeted, "If you can
offer your support, then offer your silence." She was saying this in ref-
erence to mental health support, but I thought it resonated so well
on multiple levels, including motherhood.

I'm embarrassed to admit that before I had a baby, I totally judged
other moms without even knowing what it was like to in fact be a mom.
I still cringe thinking about this. When you enter motherhood, you are
welcomed into a sisterhood unlike any other. At least, that is how I felt.
All moms have this innate bond and connection, which is why I'm sin-
cerely confused when one mom passes judgment on another.

I actually experienced mom-shaming when I was still pregnant –
not even a physical mom yet. It's real and when it is judgment o

your parenting or mothering skills, it can feel debilitating. You don't know what your one comment can do to someone on a regular day, let alone when they have raging hormones. I'll let you in on an insider tip: the unknown weight of your opinion isn't worth the gamble.

When you feel the urge to share something critical with a new mom, or soon-to-be mom, my advice would be to replace that with, "You are doing a great job", or "You're going to be a great mom." Boom. Done. You'd be surprised how far those few words can go, and this time, you've redirected your potentially hurtful comment toward something encouraging. If that mom wants your opinion, she'll ask for it. Until then, stay positive.

We're trying. We're trying our absolute hardest to do what we think is best for us, our children, our family, and our future. Our minds are constantly going, constantly worrying, and constantly feeling that mom guilt creeping in no matter what we do. In non-COVID times ... give the next mom you see a hug. She might really need it.

3. Find the right #MomTribe for you.

I knew finding a group of mom friends was important, but I didn't know how important it was to find the right mom group. I was very fortunate to have a few close friends who had babies all around the same time. I had a built-in mom club going into this! Unfortunately, those friends weren't very close in physical proximity. So, I wanted to find a local mom group as well. I tried out a few, had a couple playdates, and eventually found some mom-friends that I am incredibly grateful for.

If your babies are close in age (bonus points if they are the exact same age), your life will change having those one or two friends. The bond you form over going through the same milestones at similar times, or those worried texts of "... *This app says he should be doing this by now, but he's not! Is yours?*" And the immediate relieving answer of, *"Mine's not either!"* So you can both let out a sigh of relief because you're not alone and your baby is seconds away from the supposed milestone that this random app is telling you about, and you should just calm the fuck down because your baby is the best thing ever and totally healthy and go get that glass of wine because life is magical and everything is fine — you know ... those friends. YOU NEED THOSE FRIENDS, GIRLFRIEND! I'm also raising my hand to be this friend for you. Seriously. Reach out any time, and I will be your fellow mom cheerleader!

When you find that right mom tribe, your motherhood experience just levels right up.

4. When your baby starts to sleep through the night, it's friggin MAGICAL.

Okay. Two things from my "new mom" experience that were legit magical AF:

■. The first shower you have in your own bathroom, after pushing out an actual human being.

■ The first time you and your baby sleep through the night ... *and then you wake up in an immediate panic because you think something is wrong but then you realize that your sleep training worked and you're a badass mama.*

Let's also clear up this super annoying saying that always comes from a random uncle when he congratulates you, "Welcome to never sleeping again!" Wrong-oh, Uncle Darren. Wrong. Oh. It's called sleep training. It exists for a reason. Not every parent is down for this — that's cool! You do you, Mama! Just saying ... if sleep is something you are struggling with and something you want back, there are peeps for that.

We sleep trained Humphrey the second we could and boy oh boy, I am happy we did. He has been a magical sleeper ever since. I actually became so obsessed with sleep that I got certified as a sleep trainer and started my own consulting agency, The Rested Ranch.

I never knew how powerful and impactful sleep really was, until I became a mom. Most of your baby's mental and physical development happens when they're snoozing! I won't bore you with all of the nerdy things that I learned about how amazing sleep is — the point is, Uncle Darren was wrong.

5. Your body is fucking incredible-own it!

I'm ashamed to say that it took having a baby to reveal to me how incredible our bodies are. Yes, I attended elementary school. Yes, I also attended high school. Don't look at me like that! I know what our bodies are capable of — okay? It just took living through it and experiencing it firsthand, that really showed me, I, MYSELF... I was capable of this!

Let's just take a second to appreciate this. Our bodies are so smart and powerful that they form a human life, give birth to that life, and then, if you're lucky enough, naturally produce liquid gold to sustain and nourish that little human. THAT is what we need to focus more on, and not how much weight you might have gained in the process of creating that life.

I was so concerned about how much weight I was gaining when was pregnant. How was I going to lose all of this? Will I "bounce back"? Will I "bounce back" quickly? These were questions running through my mind every day. WHY? Honestly, how terrible is that when you think about it? I'm growing a human life, I'm exhausted, and all I can think about is how much weight I'm gaining? WTF! (If you're new, WTF stands for "Why The Face" ... Modern Family told me.) I look back and just want to give myself a hug and focus on the mind-blowing capabilities that my body has, instead of what was on the scale. It also didn't help that our society is so ingrained in this mentality that we don't even realize when we're contributing to it. I'll give you an example. If you've been pregnant or are pregnant right now, just think about how many people say things like, "Wow, you look great!" or "You're so teeny!" or "Whoa, I bet he's going to be a big baby!" While innocent comments, I'm sure, they're all talking about the same thing — how much weight you've gained.

I remember sending my sister pictures of other moms who had babies and weeks later, or sometimes days, they literally looked like a bikini model. I was so sad that I would never be like them and thought how lucky they were to have bodies like *that*.

why. **T**he. **F**ace. You know?

It literally took until the moment I had Humphrey for me to realize how incredible my body is. That living, breathing, crying, bundle of pure joy was just inside of me — and I pushed him out? From that moment forward, I actually learned what it felt like to TRULY not care about my tummy rolls or extra weight that I may be carrying around. I always said that I didn't really care about what's on the scale, but now feeling that is completely different.

I now buy clothes that actually fit me instead of buying clothes that I want to fit into. And that, my friends, is a game-changer. Why? Because who gives a flying burrito about this media-crafted perception of what it means to "bounce back"? If this term has to exist, how about we give it a different meaning? How about we think of "bouncing back" as saying goodbye to the unpleasantries of being pregnant. Bye-bye swollen feet! Bye-bye prenatal acne! Bye-bye lightning crotch! (Yeah google it. Literally the worst and just as it sounds.)

Give yourself a hug and always remember how miraculous your body is.

Motherhood opened my eyes to the actual meaning of "living your life." I mean truly living it. I mean not giving a shit about what people think of you, and just going for every single thing that you want

Humphrey opened my eyes to THIS. Time fucking flies. As cliché as it is to say, it could not be more true. So, make it count. If it's going to go by fast, it might as well be the best friggin' time ever.

I also learned that too many blueberries can make their poop black, but we can save that story for another day.

Key Takeaway

Reflect on this author's work and write down one key idea,
concept, or theme that you can take with you in your own life! If
something really hit home, connect with the author and get social!

....
....
....
....
....
....
....
....
....
....
....
....
....
....
....
....
....
....

Chapter 25
Christina Walsh

Author Photo: Cheryl Voigt - Grinning Weasel Photography
Find Christina:

@themombabes | www.themombabes.com | The Mom-Babe Podcast

H i, I'm Christina. I'm Mom to two girls ages seven and one-and-a-half. Did I plan to have kids five-and-a-half years apart? No, the universe planned it that way. Do I often get asked if they have the same dad? Yes. Surprise! They have the same dad.

The world blessed me with two little girls here on earth and one little boy in heaven. He was born at 17 weeks premature and our little William Bravery was born under almost a full moon. Just like when looking up you wouldn't see a piece missing, you wouldn't see a piece missing from our family.

My journey through motherhood started off pretty cliché: married, pregnant, new house, and baby all in one year. I took my one year of maternity leave and went back to work full time.

I loved being a working mom but when I lost my job after we lost our son, I had more grief at the time from losing my job than losing our son. It still stings when I say it. I felt I had lost my identity as I had labeled myself as this one type of person.

I got pregnant again and at 37 weeks my dad passed away and again I felt my world unravel.

Now a mom of two girls five-and-a-half years apart, I was a new mom all over again.

I have a wonderful circle of girlfriends who love my kids as much as I do, but when the postpartum fog lifted, I was going to need someone to hang out with and 'Mommy & Me' classes as a second-time mom weren't really jiving. I didn't care how much your baby weighed at birth or if they were sleeping through the night — they're babies, they don't. I wanted to know about you. The mom. Who are you? What do you like to do? What did you do before you became a mom?

So, I posted my address on the local community bulletin board with a post-it saying; *I have coffee and donuts, want a friend? Come over.* All the self-doubt crept in, was I a total loser?

The next morning, I hit the Tim Hortons drive-thru and bought a box of coffee and two dozen donuts and my doorbell rang. Moms and babies. Thirteen moms showed up that day. And the next week and the next week. It was conversation with connection.

My sister was also a new mom and we never imagined we would be on maternity leave together; we knew this was our opportunity to do *something together*.

We created the *MomBabes*. It's an online platform for moms to connect because this is what I've learned in motherhood so far: **We're better together.** We can have it all; we don't have to do it all.

I currently live with my husband and two girls in Squamish, British Columbia, a little mountain town just north of Vancouver. I love coffee, McDonald's cheeseburgers, and Dolly Parton. Here are five things that I've learned through my motherhood journey, so far.

1. You're not just a Mom.

I missed a lot of moments being a working mom and for a while, I was okay with that. The second time around I wanted to turn "maternity leave into eternity leave" but I didn't want to lose my professional identity. I wanted to continue my professional development and not feel like I'd put my career "on hold" for a year.

I wanted more; I wanted both. Can't we have it all?

No doubt motherhood has changed me and my children are everything, but I'm going to say it ...

Being a mom wasn't enough for me.

I wanted to change the rules. I wanted both. On my terms. I believe we can have both.

Whether you're at home, at a desk, or a hustling mompreneur, Mama, you gotta get out of the cheap seats and into the arena. We are talented, intelligent, capable women who had accomplishments pre-baby and need to continue to pursue our goals and dreams now

There will be time to sit on the sidelines and cheer but we need to get in the game too. Motherhood raises the stakes. Continue your own personal growth, self-care, and passion projects. Be an interesting person, probably the person you were before motherhood (remember her?) but then got swept into the world of potty training, Paw Patrol, and taxi driver.

If I want my girls to stick it out, dust themselves off after falling or their faces, or failing a test, then I had better be up for a challenge.

My kids deserve a mom worth bragging about.

2. Ask for friendship.

Remember in elementary school when you asked your friend to come over after school? Why did we stop asking?

It's not easy to find women who will love you and your kids so when you do, scoop them up. I found mine and one night over shooters and nachos (because that's how all big decisions in friendships are made) ... we were inked. Promising each other that we're in it for life.

But here's the thing... these girls are truly some of the greatest women I've ever met. We would never have all met in our teen years as we span a decade in ages; it's crazy how age doesn't matter as we get older. We just have that fierce lady friendship where we aggressively believe in each other, defend each other, and cheer each other on. No judgment, just the 24-hour text chat where we can vent, cry, talk in GIFS and laugh until it hurts or send out that 911 text when you need to drop off your kid or need to pop in for a glass of wine ... or two.

We've been bridesmaids in each other's weddings, supported each other through separations, moves, pregnancies, loss of babes, loss of parents, starting new businesses, graduations ... and a whole lot of birthday parties (16 kids in total). My favourite thing to tell them is that we may not have all grown up together, but we all get to grow old together.

You don't need seven, maybe it's just one ... but you need to find those friends to do life with whether you're a mom or not. Life is supposed to be done through community and sometimes you have to be brave and create what you want to be a part of. Put yourself out there. Have you been invited to something new? Go. Did you sign up for a Mommy & Me class? Talk to the mom next to you. Join a gym, go to yoga, talk to your barista ... or hey, call up that friend or slide into their DMs (whatever the kids are doing these days), and reconnect. You just never know where you may meet your girl gang.

And just ask them to come over. I bet they will say yes. They don't care about dirty dishes; they care about you!

3. Throw out all your underwear.

I did a crazy thing after babies. I threw out all my underwear.

The postpartum Walmart undies had to go. Like, let's not hold on to those for another five years. Now, commando may be your thing (you're cooler than me) but I'm a bikini brief kinda gal myself.

Underwear is like this strange time capsule of life. And do you really throw underwear out? Nope. You keep those neon green undies you bought at La Senza in college because ... *why? The memories? Hah!*

Now if you say to your girlfriend, "I threw out all my underwear and bought 25 pairs of comfy cotton briefs" and they say, "Oh I could never do that! My husband loves sexy underwear!"

Hah. Again. I beg to differ.

Your husband doesn't care what underwear you have because he doesn't want you wearing underwear. And hear me on this, YOU are the sexy one. Not the underwear.

So go, dig out those undies. Open the drawer and dump it out and say goodbye to the postpartum panties, neon thongs, too stretched, too small ratty old undies.

Here's your permission slip to go buy new ones. All cotton, all comfortable, all body parts can be tucked in if necessary.

My morning routine feels so much better. I feel prettier, more comfortable and strangely put together.

Life is like underwear. Change is good.

4. The juggle struggle.

Let me let you in on a little secret because you will hear it over and over: *find the balance.* And here's the truth salad: **the scale is never going to be even.**

Whether you're a working mom, stay-at-home mom, work-from

home mom — whatever crown you carry you will look for balance. And the scale will continue to tip back and forth, life will ebb and flow, and you have to ride the wave of the season.

You will learn what you can control and what you can't. Also here's another helping of truth salad: you can't control it all.

The juggle is real. Like a real-life game of Twister.

Right-hand blue, left-hand red.

I've done the juggle.

The morning juggle.

The workday juggle

The childcare juggle.

The "I'm-going-to-do-my-master's-degree-now" juggle.

The bedtime-with-a-newborn juggle.

Mama, I've done the "juggle struggle," and here's the thing: I don't really believe this whole "work-life-mom-all-the-things" balance. Kinda makes me twitch. Some seasons are more like Twister and we're juggling bouncy balls that bounce right back. And sometimes the season is just hard. Balls drop. We pick them up or we push them under the couch. Either is okay.

We're surviving what feels almost impossible some days but we keep going, keep juggling, AND keep going. Then all of a sudden you survived the impossible. Right foot green, left-hand blue. Not impossible.

Just know that you can always throw a few balls to another mama. We're on the same team.

5. "World's Okayest Mom" (...and I'm okay with that.)

Remember that saying, "Mom knows best"? Well, there is some solid truth to that. You know your kid. Trust that.

In a world of Dr. Google, a million mom forums and curated Instagram feeds, it's so easy to get caught up in "Am I doing this right?"

It's as easy as overhearing two moms chatting in a Mommy & Me group, or a random woman in the grocery store giving you her opinion like its gospel — to second guess yourself.

You don't have to follow the rules; you don't have to follow anything.

I remember when someone said to me, "I would never want a December baby. Having a baby in winter is not fun. When is your baby's birthday?"

"December."

I'm thinking, I will snuggle in winter and in summer she can crawl around, it will be great. Well, joke's on me. My baby couldn't even sit come summer.

P.S. You can't curate motherhood.

My oldest slept in a crib until age four, and I have never bought a potty. One had bottles until three, we still have to talk about thumb-sucking, and one has a soother that I have yet to even think about setting on fire. It's as easy as: "Good for her, not for me."

I want to reassure you that everything will be okay. You will doubt yourself, worry, lose sleep, and probably give yourself grey hair. But believe me, you've got this.. You're raising a HUMAN and mamas have done this for millions of years all while running the world and cleaning up the kitchen.

Remember, they all get to kindergarten potty trained.

I want you to know that the best version of you means that you are doing the best you can. You are doing enough and we don't have to be perfect to be good moms. There's no "World's Best Mom" mug here. We're enough, and that's enough.

Enough said.

Key Takeaway

Reflect on this author's work and write down one key idea, concept, or theme that you can take with you in your own life! If something really hit home, connect with the author and get social!

....
....
....
....
....
....
....
....
....
....
....
....
....
....
....
....
....
....

Chapter 26
Carolyn Turkington

Author Photo: Cheryl Voigt - Grinning Weasel Photography
Find Carolyn:
@themombabes | www.themombabes.com | The MomBabe Podcast

I always knew I'd be a boy mom, but what I didn't realize is how motherhood would change my life. I had preeclampsia during my pregnancy that went undiagnosed and untreated leading to a myriad of problems, multiple surgeries, and permanent hear damage. My son was born not breathing and after spending time i the NICU followed by a surgery of his own, our first days were not th way I had imagined. No fancy newborn photos, skin to skin cuddle or pretty maternity robes over here, just mesh underwear, projectil formula barf, and staring at my son through plexiglass.

I felt I was grieving the loss of the "perfect" motherhood experienc that had been ripped away from me when I would now be thrown int the deep end with the passing of my dad at three months postpartur

I really believe I was given the choice to either crumble or to climb ... and I chose to climb. To say it was f*cking hard is a bit of an understatement, but I knew sitting in the thickness of my grief wouldn't help me, and it wouldn't feed my son.

I knew I had "to do" something and one night over some meal planning and a glass of wine, my sister and I came to the agreement that we "need to do something more." Our dad was a man of the community. He really was the modern-day George Bailey, knowing everyone by name and helping everyone he could. His gift to us was leaving us both with this innate ability to know that life isn't about that trip you will "one day" take; it's about the everyday and who you have alongside you enjoying the everyday mess along the way. Because let's be honest, life is messy.

So, we created an online community called the *MomBabes*, where we lead women to show up as their best — or as their messy — selves because both are enough. It's simple: moms want more and we are running the world all while cleaning up the kitchen.

I'm living every day with my whole heart and my whole ass! Because babes, I don't half-ass anything!

Two years ago, I thought I had lost myself but I didn't lose myself in motherhood; I found myself.

***

Hi, I'm Carolyn and I live in a town whose claim to fame is having cheap gas! I live with my husband, our two-year-old son, and our labradoodle, Ollie. I'm a teacher by day and a podcast host by night. I'm a jump-in-with-two-feet, swing-for-the-fences kinda gal. I live for hot coffee, McDonald's fries, and I love a good deal!

Here are the *5 Lessons* I've learned in my short season of motherhood.

1. Choose you!

"Love yourself as fiercely as you love them," has stuck with me. Not sure if it's a Pinterest quote or maybe I can take credit but, in all seriousness, I would do anything for my kid, so why not myself?

I'm now a mother who mothers myself first.

The term self-care is this tossed around buzzword and I used to get tired of hearing it. But that's because I wasn't making time to care for myself.

Now I think of self-care as my permission slip; I don't need to go the extra mile to find time for me. We are often judged for taking the time, and we don't listen to the smoke signals until our mind and body are screaming at us from the inside out. Manicures, haircuts, bubble baths, and those weekly Starbucks can make us feel good, but self-care is more than "feel good" moments. It's a connection to the thing you are doing.

I learned to not let society, motherhood blogs, or random people label my basic needs as luxurious activities. Taking a shower is not self-care, it is a basic need.

As a new mom I used to say, "Oh, I just don't have time for myself!" But that's now shifted to me giving myself the permission to ask, "What do I need right now?"

**Choosing the time to invest in yourself,
then advocating for it — this is self-care.**

Choosing YOU is mandatory. It is choosing to do the things that you can't do when your kid is awake. So, it's not cleaning the house, prepping dinner, or answering emails. I do all of those things, but I can empty the dishwasher and do laundry when my kid is awake. What I can't do is write, or sleep, complete a workout, or drink hot coffee. I do the things that bring me joy and I have learned to fulfill my own personal needs with intention.

We always have a choice. Here's your permission slip to say yes to yourself, your needs, wants, and desires. Start with 10 minutes per day.

You deserve this.

2. Just put the damn suit on!

F L A W S O M E // adj. A rad woman who embraces her "flaws" but knows that she's awesome regardless.

Raise your hand if you love this!

As a new mom, FOMO[6] is real and I wasn't about to miss out on ALL the fun. I'm hitting the beach and the waterslide. I'm showing my son that women's bodies are all sizes — and that I'm one of them. Because celebrating every-BODY is something that I can really get be-HIND.

Size 6 or 16, our babes just want us in the pool, not on the sidelines. I've got babes to inspire so I'm getting out there with every fold, dimple, and stretch mark.

Don't fall down the Instagram rabbit hole of comparison and self-loathing. We are overloaded with "curated perfection" and I'm soooo over it. How about a little shape, some curve, and a whole lot of melons!

So, do me a favour ... be brave and put the suit on! No one is looking at you thinking, "What is that mama doing?" We are our own worst critics #truth.

All our kids care about is that their mom was there. Making waves, splashing, and soaking up the fun. So, don't let this summer, or any season, be the one where you sit in the shade because you're scared to wear shorts! #notthisyear Make waves ... a whole lot of them!

Motherhood comes in every shape, size, and struggle. No two jour-

According to the Oxford Dictionary, Fear of missing out (FOMO) is anxiety that an exciting or interesting event may currently be happening elsewhere, often aroused by posts seen on social media. Accessed November 5, 2020, www.lexico.com/en/definition/fomo

neys are the same, so own it! You're one in a big beautiful juicy melon!

Let's go, mamas!

Sun's out, cheeks out!

It's time we got the tan lines, baked our muffin tops, and made the memories we all deserve to have.

Let's all be Flawsome together.

3. Set the boundary; You're not a bitch; You're a badass!

Are you a woman without boundaries? Isn't it exhausting?

As a recovering people pleaser, I learned that feeling overworked, tired, and guilty was actually a result of me having zero boundaries and not having a clue of what type of woman I wanted to be.

But now as a mom, if I didn't learn some personal boundaries quickly, motherhood would soon take control of me.

Boundaries are meant to protect you, but boundaries don't have to be hard or permanent lines. Boundaries shift and evolve how you do since you're the one setting them. Your network will start respecting your yeses and noes when you do. This is your race, so you set the pace. You must stay in your lane, meaning this work is on you. You must get clear on what you want, what you need, what fuels you, and what brings you joy. Then do it and do it on *purpose*.

Stop comparing yourself to other moms. They aren't you. You are you, and you do you.

For me, it took a lot of *listening* to myself and paying attention to what made me light up and where I needed to dig deeper — to answer those questions with clear intentions. Once I knew what I wanted, I could start placing boundaries where I needed to.

You can't have a wishbone in the place where you need to have a backbone. Mamas, it's simple: boundaries are self-love.

4. The power of affirmations.

"Have a birth plan," they said. I LOVE a good plan, so plan I did. I took all the prenatal classes, packed all the bags, and I even got my nails done. What I didn't know is that the plan can go to total sh*t in about 2.2 seconds and you are left feeling scared sh*tless. I wish I had had one person say to me, "Hey it's good to have a plan, but know that you most likely won't follow it."

A few hours after my son was born, while we waited for the helicopter to transfer him to the NICU, I lied my way out of recovery saying my pain was only a 5/10 when in reality it was about a 9, but I just had to see my baby. I got to see him for about five minutes before he was flown away, and I never would have thought that this was going to be our start. Our story. If I had only known what was ahead for us, I think I would have given him a better pep talk than I did.

Babies are so much more resilient than we give them credit for, and I owe it to my son who showed me firsthand what it truly meant to *be brave* and resilient to whatever comes our way.

A saying that I repeat daily, heck multiple times a day, got me through all those uncertain and unbearable moments. But adopting the two words that would inevitably be the last words that my dad told me before he passed, and it's what my son shows me every day... *Be brave*.

Mamas, just be brave.

Motherhood is tough, but so are you.

Find the words that you can hold on to, wholeheartedly believe and breathe in.

5. Tit for tat - ain't no time for that.

Resentment is real. FOMO is real. As new moms, our daily life, our schedule, *everything* is flipped upside down.

However, often our partners don't have to make the same adjustments in their day to day because they're still going to work and hitting the gym while you're "stuck" at home with a newborn. Or my personal favourite: he takes 45 minutes to go poop, and you're wrangling the kids and trying to cook dinner.

Mama, I get it. Here's the secret: communication.

Tell them that you need their help. Tell them how they can help and then ask nicely.

They cannot read our minds. You have to tell them. Tell them what you need. Tell them that you need to have a shower. Ask them if they can clean up the dishes (even if they load the dishwasher wrong or put everything in the wrong size Tupperware). This shit doesn't matter. It matters that together you're tackling the day. Tell them that they can have a beer with the boys because trust me, they feel the daily stresses too, it's just different. Don't complain about them to other women or say how "easy" they have it. You can have it too. As them for what you need and then go do it.

Don't keep score. Marriage and parenthood are never equal. Remember that you are a team and that everyone will get their turn. And my favourite, ask the babysitter!

Date your partner on a regular basis.

Whether it's going for dinner, hitting the gym, or going to the local bar on a Saturday night and getting college drunk again! You will probably talk about the kids the whole time, but quality and uninterrupted time together is always worth it. Finish off the night with a good make-out sesh, but be careful ... that could turn into more babies.

Key Takeaway

Reflect on this author's work and write down one key idea, concept, or theme that you can take with you in your own life! If something really hit home, connect with the author and get social!

Chapter 27

Samantha Archer

Find Samantha: @samantha.archer

've always had an interest in writing and the material I gravitate toward reading is always when a person is sharing their story. I love it when someone can write down their experiences and we as the reader get to connect to that person and learn from where they've been.

When I first heard about this project, I immediately wanted to participate. I mean, I'm a mom of a five and three-year-old and I chose to stay home and devote myself to mothering full-time when my first was born. My full-time job is being a mama, and I absolutely love that this project allowed me to think back on the last six years and revisit all the highs and lows and the incredible lessons that I've learned along the way.

Before staying home, I was an Early Childhood Educator with a degree in Psychology, so I felt pretty prepared for my own children. Once my son arrived, I realized that it was harder to have your own child full-time versus having a group of 10 where you get to clock out at some point during the day. My oldest started school this past September and it was uncharted waters for us. We had been together since I was pregnant and it was hard to let him go. I realized then what a compliment it was of my working families to say that they felt comfortable leaving their child in my care. It was an absolute honour to be a part of the village that helped to raise their children. Parenting is tough and takes a village. I feel like all of the mamas in this book are a part of the village, reaching out to all of the readers. I'm so happy that you're here! Here are the lessons that I've learned along my motherhood journey so far.

You embark on this crazy journey called pregnancy: nine months of roller-coaster emotions, hormones, cravings, weight gain, morning (read: ALL DAY) sickness, swollen ankles, waddling like a duck, and all kinds of other super fun symptoms. Phew. So, after that lovely little intro, of course, you're like WHY NOT? Honestly, I've done it twice and I don't regret it at all. But it is FAR from easy — at least, it was not easy for me. I didn't enjoy pregnancy one bit. Once those nine months (that feel like forty-seven, hello third trimester!) are over, the fun begins.

Here's your baby! Just go on and take that little, itty, bitty human home, and keep it alive! Bye! I had an extended hospital stay with my first. We didn't go home until five days after his birth. But whether you leave a day, a week, or a month after you give birth with your first child... it is scary. I had a dog, but I mean, this is a human we are talking about. Can't just put down a food dish and leave for the day, y'know? I felt super nervous. Which brings us to the first lesson I learned through motherhood:

1. You've got this, Mama!

You're going to learn alongside your baby. Whether breast or bottle-fed, co-sleeping or not, you'll get into a rhythm as a team. For the first three months, it was like learning to dance. My son and I stepped on each other's toes, we wept, we got frustrated and each day just kept coming. By his third month here and my third month as a mom, we had a rhythm down. We had routines. I had showers. He had actual windows of sleep. Like anything you do in life, there's a learning curve, but you're capable and together you'll thrive. That mother-child bond is innate and it will be your guiding force.

With my second, I felt much more confident in myself because I realized the first time around, I was able to do this thing called parenting. Every cry didn't cause alarm, and I'd already done the trial and error thing. It was easier to be calmer and just trust that I had this.

2. Motherhood Teaches you confidence.

Everyone has opinions, and lots of people feel compelled to share them — even when they're not wanted. Let all that unsolicited advice go in one ear and exit out the other. Motherhood teaches you confidence. You know your child the very best and you're their advocate. Don't let anyone make you second guess your ability as you child's mom. It is easy to feel judged for the decisions you make as a mother for your family. Don't waver, Mama! You've got this. Having this little person who depends on you for their survival ends up teaching you to be bold and confident, even if you're usually shy and quiet. That confident feeling is one of the very best.

3. Be flexible.

If you're a Type A Personality like I am, then this next lesson is going to be a hard pill to swallow. Be flexible. Plan all you want. Write it all down. Just know that even the best-laid plans are going to get derailed by your sweet little bundles of chaos. I was always punctual. Early by an acceptable amount to all appointments, outings, events — then I had kids and I've been on time maybe five times in as many years. If you think you've covered all your bases, it is best to keep in the back of your mind that there's always one thing that you didn't plan for. Kids have a way!

This isn't to scare you, fellow Type A-ers, it is just to let you know that it is totally okay when it seems like your world has come unhinged a little bit. Adjust your sails and go, Mama. You might not feel like it at the moment, but you'll appreciate learning the art of flexibility. You'll be calmer and ready to roll with the punches in a way that you haven't been before now.

4. You NEED "you time."

So now I'll share the hardest lesson that I've learned along the way: you NEED you time. My son's birth was traumatic. I had HELLP Syndrome[6] — recovery was rough. I was not able to separate from my son. My separation anxiety made things that used to be so incredibly common and easy, like grocery shopping, near impossible with me sitting in the driveway trying to leave and then rushing back home. The time away wasn't easy for me. I was consumed. And, that can unfortunately result in exhaustion. An exhausted mom isn't the best mom. So, not

Preeclampsia Foundation. HELLP Syndrome is a life-threatening pregnancy complication usually considered to be a variant of preeclampsia. Both conditions usually occur during the later stages of pregnancy or sometimes after childbirth. The acronym is formed by H (hemolysis, which is the breaking down of red blood cells), EL (elevated liver enzymes) and LP (low platelet count). Accessed November 6, 2020, www.preeclampsia.org/hellp-syndrome

only was I not filling my cup, it was negatively affecting my mothering. My cousin lovingly, but pushily, took me to a yoga studio. That was when my son was two. He's five now and I still practice yoga. I felt calmer after every class. Refreshed. Refocused. Ready to go home and be a mom again. Please take time for yourself — you'll never regret it. It is good to remember that you're still you. You aren't only a mother and you deserve to care for yourself just as passionately as you care for your kids.

5. Lead by example.

Lastly, a lesson of self-love and acceptance. It wasn't a lesson I was expecting, but it is one that I'm so grateful for. After becoming a mom (x2), I'm gentler with myself. I'm not my own worst critic anymore. Every bump, stretch mark, and physical change made me a mom. I tell my daughter that she is brave, smart, kind, strong, loving ... and I mean it. These are the qualities that I want to emphasize. I want her healthy and happy — but, not a slave to a scale, a beauty store, or someone else's ideals. It's okay to love yourself; allow yourself to take up space unapologetically. Get in the photo with your kids even if you don't have your hair done. You'll love these memories and the kids just love having their mom with them. I was always self-conscious in a bathing suit but now I put one on and get in the pool. The belly laughter, happiness, and memories I get with my children far outweigh any negative self-talk. I don't want that for my daughter so it is best to lead by example!

Becoming a mom is an amazing thing; becoming a mother makes you strong in ways you didn't even know were possible. Every birth story, child, and relationship is unique. They're all so special and you learn so much along the way. You go into it thinking that your role the teacher — but you're also the student. Your kids teach you things that you otherwise never would've known. It's an awesome journey. There are tears and frustration along the way, but your heart is going to burst out of your chest in the very best way a thousand times over.

Congratulations, Mama! You're going to love it!

Key Takeaway

Reflect on this author's work and write down one key idea,

concept, or theme that you can take with you in your own life! If

something really hit home, connect with the author and get social!

....

....

....

....

....

....

....

....

....

....

....

....

....

....

....

....

....

....

Chapter 28
Kandice Lea

Author Photo: Rachel Hamm
Find Kandice: @kandiceleaco

Hi, sweet mama, I'm Kandice Lea! A "young" mama of two, ages five and one-and-a-half, a fiancée to my dream man of 10 years, entrepreneur of nine years, coach & host of the *She Can Thrive* podcast! I'm obsessed with helping women intentionally show up, level up, and thrive in their life and their business!

I always knew that I wanted to be a mama, but I also always knew that I had big goals that I wanted to accomplish. At 19, I finished college, finished my apprenticeship, and found myself feeling a huge pull to become an entrepreneur and to create a life that truly felt good to me. I was in a chapter of being completely lost within myself and I knew I wanted more, wanted better.

I created my first business and before long it took off and every thing that I wanted was falling into place. I was finally so aligned with my vision for my life and the work I was doing.

I was 21 when we became pregnant with baby #1 and 22 when he was born. It's funny because I was definitely categorized as a "young" mom but it actually felt like the most perfect timing.

When Brayden came, the overwhelming amount of love and responsibility that I had for him, then my business and life itself, brought me to experiencing anxiety for the first time in my life — I mean, finding balance can be hard AF!

How was I going to master this? How was this going to all work out like it had before? How was I going to keep it all together? My boobs hurt, the laundry is piling up and my email inbox might actually explode!

Finding balance in our new normal wasn't a breeze, but like all things as a mama — you push through and it does actually happen and get easier)! Remember, you are never alone and this stage you may be in right now — it won't last forever!

1. Asking for help doesn't mean that you aren't capable.

I know you've been told this. I know you've maybe even thought about doing it ... and then you decided not to. As a new mama, entrepreneur, and recovering perfectionist — I burned myself out more times than I can count out of fear and worry about what others would think of me.

It took me about 17 months of multitasking, burnout, and honestly just losing a connection that I once had with myself, before I realized that if I wanted to be the mama, the wife, frig, even the human being that I wanted to be — that asking for help didn't mean that I wasn't capable of doing alone, it meant that I was strong enough to know what I wanted and needed.

This likely feels different for all mamas, but if you're currently strug-gling and looking at the laundry that needs to be folded, the house that is upside down, and the dishes in the sink (don't stress, mine has looked the same!), but you're not asking for help, I encourage you to ask another mama, grandmama, or someone you can trust to just come and hang out while you do what you feel you need to do.

My note to my past self: Start asking for help before you desper-ately need it. What you are doing is hard work and you deserve help.

2. "Ugh. I don't have the mental energy to go."

But I'd pack up and off we went anyway!

It took having my second baby and experiencing a lot of person-al development for me to start setting boundaries and saying "NO" when I intuitively just knew I could not flipping handle it and that it was OKAY TO SAY NO!

I'm going to share a phrase with you that a loved one shared with me exactly when I needed it most: "You don't owe anyone an expla-nation for doing what feels best for you or your little ones."

Set those boundaries, do what feels good, and STOP doing what doesn't feel good!

I started saying no (maybe more than I should have, now that I'm enjoying the benefits of boundaries haha) and I stopped allowing myself to get caught up in the thoughts that others might have and the anxiety slowly decreased!

My note to my past self: Only you can truly take care of your per-sonal needs. By setting boundaries, you'll be better for yourself and your family.

3. Patience in my back pocket.

Patience with me, with them, and everything in between.

When I was a kid, my parents would ask what I had in my pocket when leaving the house, and I would have to respond with "manners." These days I'm leaving with patience in my pocket ... *a LOT* of it!

I honestly was always worried that I wouldn't have the patience to "mom," always wondering how I'd get things done or keep it "all together." Fast forward a few years and a baby later, and I realized that we're not ever going to have it all together, and that it's actually totally okay to accept and embrace that. But what has helped the most is understanding that patience develops, and the more I remind myself of where these little people are coming from (through the meltdowns, the booboos, the sleepless nights, and the tears when I leave) it's helped me to see that though I don't have it all together, it can be done without as much chaos as I imagined — as long as I keep my patience in my back pocket, LOL!

My note to my past self: By bringing patience into your life, you teach patience to others and events can play out differently. On the days where patience is lacking, follow step one and ask for help or support where it's needed.

4. A bad day, moment, choice, or action doesn't make you a bad mom.

Depending on what stage of mama-hood you're in with your littles, you either know exactly what I'm about to talk about, or maybe this is something you can take forward with you.

Those days that are never-ending, when there isn't enough coffee in the world, or the times when you feel embarrassed, ashamed, upset, or sometimes even frustrated by an action, word, or choice made by your little, does NOT define YOU as their mama.

As a first-time mama, this was something that was hard for me to swallow. I remember beating myself up because of a choice or word that was made by my firstborn when he was old enough to realize that he too could make choices for himself. I would get so worked up that it would happen again. What would others think of him — or MY parenting? What had I done wrong? How could I "fix" it?

The reality is that you can't just "fix" every situation. These little humans are growing and evolving just as we are. Just like us, they are going to learn through trial and error and it may not always end up the way WE as the mama might want it to — but we do hold the ability to see it from a different perspective and to help them navigate their choices.

My note to my past self: Don't put so much pressure on yourself or the situations happening around you, Mama, for you are evolving and so are they.

5. Take five, Mama, and skip the guilt.

I know you've probably heard this half a dozen times, but I actually mean it.

It's hard stuff that you're doing and you are always wearing more than one hat (if not five, am I right?). I remember getting to the point where I felt like I was suffocating in kids, messes, tasks, work, and then the things that we had to attend. It took me learning all of the above lessons (and then some) to finally realize that I was wanting so much for my family and my babies, for myself and for our future, but I was never slowing down long enough to take a little bit of time for me, with just me.

You love these little people so damn hard; I mean you'd give up anything for them — but what if we also loved ourselves that way?

And refused to give up our sanity and self-worth? I mean, it would almost be like having your cake and eating it too, wouldn't it?

So why don't we take five (or heck, 20) minutes and just be ALONE? This one habit transformation made all the difference in my life and how I raise my kids and show up for my family. I can think clearly, and I've had time alone before anyone wakes up and requires my help and because of that, I have more grace.

Journal, walk, move your body, meditate, clean, sip a hot coffee, listen to music, roll the windows down and belt out your favourite song. Just do something every single day — for you!

My note to my past self: If you practice just taking 5–20 minutes a day entirely for yourself, by yourself, you will feel like a better version of yourself, and then you can show up better for them as well.

XO

Key Takeaway

Reflect on this author's work and write down one key idea,

concept, or theme that you can take with you in your own life! If

something really hit home, connect with the author and get social!

....
....
....
....
....
....
....
....
....
....
....
....
....
....
....
....
....
....

Chapter 29

Jessie Lammers

Author Photo: Frolic + Bloom Photography
Find Jessie: @cultivating.self.ish

Most days, my "best" consists of dry Lucky Charms and ha
brushed hair. Getting my three children out the door an
praying they have shoes on in the car. Making my way t
the coffee shop to check off three of the ten things on my work to-d
list. Dinner and dishes and dodging my middle child when she ask
me to play horses for the tenth time. Slipping into bed at night an
watching the laundry basket taunt me in the corner, clean clothe
heaping over, left unfolded another day. My kids jumping in be
next to me and fighting over who will lay on my arm until I drift int
exhaustion only to wake up and do it again the next day. I've been
mother for over six years and most days I feel like I have no clue wha
I'm doing.

1. I am not a good mom.

Somewhere between tying my shoes and learning the ABC's, I learned how to be a good girl. As the youngest on both sides of a blended family, I learned what not to do from my rebellious older siblings. When I was a kid, my mom would ask me, "You aren't going to turn into a mean teenager, are you? You're my sweet girl." I would always reassure her that I was good and would always be good and sweet and easy.

I carried this identity into adulthood. I loved being loved by everyone. I loved doing what I "should" be doing. I loved making the right decision. Then I got pregnant and the right decision wasn't so clear. Conflicting advice rolled in from every direction. Bottle feed. Breastfeed. Vaccinate. Don't. Co-sleep. Don't you dare put that baby in your bed! What I should do to be a good mother was about as clear as the skies in Forks, Washington during a *Twilight movie*.

Still, I held on to this "good girl" persona like it was my job. But then I got pregnant with my second child. I was anxious and exhausted all the time. I frantically made decisions and then changed my mind. Trying to please everyone and be a mom was tearing me apart. I couldn't please everyone and most days, I pleased no one.

I had to shed some of my good girl persona to forge my own path in motherhood. I quit listening to everyone else so that I could hear my own voice. I recently read *Untamed* by Glennon Doyle and this passage stood out to me: "We forget how to know, when we learn how to please." Her words spilled tears down my cheeks.

I didn't realize that I was carrying this burden until I became a mother. I didn't want it anymore. More than that, I didn't want my girls to feel like they had to carry that burden to be a good mom. So, I traded that title for one that felt truer to me. I don't always do what other people want me to do. I don't have it all together, and I certainly don't please everyone anymore. I don't do what I'm "supposed to do" and if that makes me a "not good" mom, I'll wear that badge with honour.

2. Motherhood hurts.

My first year of motherhood was filled with pain. Upon finding out that I was pregnant, one of the first decisions I made was to breast-feed. I thought it would be easy because it was natural, so I was un-prepared for the challenges we were both going to face. The first night in the hospital, post-birth, I screamed hysterically at the nurses to bring me formula. My baby wouldn't latch, but I knew she was hungry. For the record, natural is not always easier. When we made it home, our fight was far from over. Our first 10 months were filled with breast pumps and cracked nipples, supply issues, and lactation consultants. By the time my supply dried up, I could proudly say that I had suffered through more physical pain than I had ever collective-ly experienced in my 22 years.

My first year of motherhood also brought some of the most in-tense emotions I had ever felt. I tell people all the time that I loved my baby so much it hurt. I felt everything more deeply. When I was away from her, my heart ached. When she was sick, I felt physically ill. Even the good feelings were too much to hold in my body. Earli-er this year, she competed in her first cheer competition. Watching her on stage, performing, having fun, being part of a team, filled me with a sense of pride so big, I thought I would explode.

Then there was the postpartum depression. My doctor had warned me about it but I didn't notice its presence until I was sob-bing on the floor of Target. My mom and sister had to physically pick me up and take me home; I don't even remember what set me off. My love for my baby was so overwhelming, I felt nothing for anyone else. Emotions crippled me and I felt worthless for how little I was able to accomplish. I didn't think I was worthy of the amount of love that surrounded me. I had never understood people who wanted to commit suicide until those days.

Even now, the words are hard to write but I feel like they need to be shared. If you suffer from postpartum depression, I am with you

Mama. Sometimes you will feel so alone but know that you aren't. For me, self-acceptance and my support system eventually won over the feelings. Time was my greatest ally and as stealthily as the depression had set in, it disappeared, leaving a new phase and a new obstacle in its place.

3. Flow, don't control.

Patience has never really been my virtue. I'm a product of the instant gratification era so it came as a shock to me when my kids didn't adopt my "get it done quickly" attitude. I spent months worrying/reading/praying about how I would get my firstborn off the pacifier and when my second child didn't wean from breastfeeding until I was pregnant with my third, I thought I was for sure doing something wrong.

Don't even get me started on our daily routines. At this point, I would much rather get a root canal than initiate another "out the door" or "clean up" routine. It takes sooooo long. By the time my middle child is ready, the youngest has half of his clothes off. No song, strategy, or positive behaviour approach seems to work. And trust me, I've tried it all.

Every time we face a new issue or bump in the road, you can find me knee-deep in Google searches and self-help books. I've learned a lot through Pinterest, but none of it is particularly useful for getting my way. I have reached an understanding though. Stressing over benchmarks and behaviours and what I can do to "fix" whatever problem we are facing currently is doing nothing but taking me out of the present moment. Also, typically, by the time I think I have a handle on the situation, a new issue swoops in to take up the spotlight.

I'm convinced that being a mom is kind of like living through a series of apocalypses. Each new phase feels like the end of the world but it's really just a chance to uncover something new about ourselves and our kids. We fret and fight thinking that we are helpless, only to realize that sometimes time and a whole lot of patience is all that's necessary to work it out.

4. We weren't born to live for our kids.

A well-meaning comment from a family member cut through my gut, "Your kids are only little once. Enjoy them while you can." I'd been thinking about starting my own business for a while and this was her way of telling me that doing so would take far more time away from my kids than was socially acceptable. I let this fear cripple me for years. A weekend trip away with the husband? Can't, we have kids. Dinner with friends? No, I need to spend time with the kids. Relaxing pedicure? Sure, but let me feel guilty the whole time I'm gone because the kids are probably missing me.

This guilt that I felt, while normal by today's standards, was also completely unwarranted. We aren't meant to spend every waking moment with our children. We aren't meant to put every dream, every trip, every relationship on hold until our children grow up. In fact, doing so can cause more harm than good. We are accustomed to this mother martyrdom where our kids come first, and we come last. And we're miserable. We aren't enjoying their childhood. We are living out of mom guilt and praying for nap time. We are burned out and resentful.

We are teaching our children that this is acceptable. We are teaching our children to ignore their own needs to fulfill the needs of others. I don't want to live for my kids. I want to teach them how to live. I want them to see me dreaming big. I want them to know what is possible. I want them to know that if they are choosing between making someone else happy and staying true to themselves, they are validated in doing the latter.

5. Be prepared To be wrong... repeatedly!

Before I had kids, I thought I would be a great mother because I was a great aunt. Then I became a mom and realized how wrong I was. There is a whole new level of expertise required to be solely responsible for another human being. There is no shortage of decisions to be made and a lot of times, us new moms are making these decisions blindly.

I pierced my oldest daughter's ears when she was two months old. Then I read an article about body autonomy and decided that I shouldn't be the one making that decision. Before I realized the damage that my "good girl" persona had on me, I taught my oldest how to people please. Now I cringe when she seeks reassurance that she is doing a good job and gives in to make other people happy. I've beat myself up about it, but I also now realize that as Maya Angelou said, "We don't know better until we know better and then, we can do better."

Now I reserve the right to change my mind ... a lot. I'm getting older and so are my kids. I am constantly learning and redeveloping my views on parenting and the world. I'll never be done learning and growing, but I also have to make decisions now that will affect my children. I've learned to give myself grace throughout this journey because I'm doing the best that I can with the knowledge that I have.

Most days, it takes everything in me to make it to the finish line. At night, when I don't immediately crash, I sit in bed and think of all the ways that I messed up and could do better. I recall any moments where I lost my cool or wasn't as present as I wanted to be. I worry that my kids don't feel loved or valued enough or that they don't have enough structure.

Then sometimes, I just get it. I know it's not having it all together that makes a good mom; it's not the Pinterest-worthy meals and crafts or the psychologist-approved parenting techniques. Some nights I stare at my sweet babies' faces as they sleep and thank the

Universe that I get to wake up and try again.

I wholeheartedly believe that what makes me a good mom isn't that I show up perfectly, it's that I continue to show up each day, again and again, imperfectly.

Key Takeaway

Reflect on this author's work and write down one key idea, concept, or theme that you can take with you in your own life! If something really hit home, connect with the author and get social!

....
....
....
....
....
....
....
....
....
....
....
....
....
....
....
....
....
....
....
....

#5lessons #leadherpublishing

Chapter 30
Tanis Twiddy

Find Tanis: @tanist_55

I was told I was a *geriatric* pregnancy. The other term for this is a pregnancy of *advanced maternal age* (AMA), with the latter only sounding marginally better.

By definition, a geriatric pregnancy is any pregnancy in a woman over the age of 35. As a nurse practitioner I had used this definition in my own practice to identify women who could be at an increased risk for certain pregnancy-related complications, but I never really thought about how it would feel to have the label placed on myself. I knew I wasn't in my twenties anymore, but I didn't feel *old*, and certainly not *geriatric*!

I think the label affirmed a couple of fears that I already had about motherhood, which is why it bothered me so much. It affirmed that I had wanted to become a mother long before I actually did, and it

supported the nagging question of "Did I wait too long?" It also am-
plified uncertainties that I had about whether I could even hack it
as a mom and what kind of mom I would be. Would my age be one
more thing that I had to worry about? Would my old geriatric knees
be able to keep up with the baby? While I believe now that many of
my fears surrounding pregnancy were unfounded, I've come to realize that my age has shaped a lot of my motherhood experience. For
anyone walking into motherhood at a later stage in life, which, let's
be honest, is a LOT of us, I feel that the advice I would give would be
a little different, as I believe that our experiences as *seasoned wom-
en* (as I prefer to say) are somewhat unique.

One of the biggest things that I struggled with in becoming a
mother was finding a balance between my self-identity and being
a mother. From the moment that I held my daughters in my arms, I
knew that my life had forever changed and my focus shifted almost
immediately from "me" to "them."

Overnight, my Instagram feed went from pictures of travel and
eating out to loads of pictures of my babies. My previous hobbies,
aspirations, and personal pleasures seemed to take a back seat. I
am so proud of the fact that I get to call myself a mom and all of the
positive ways that my children have impacted my life, particularly by
helping me to become a more selfless individual. But I have always
been challenged by the thought of "Who am I now?" compared to
the person I was before I had children.

I was thirty-one when I met my husband and living in a trendy
neighborhood on the west end of Toronto, Ontario. I had traveled
a fair amount, did some relief work in Haiti after the earthquake in
2011, and completed my yoga teaching certification in Costa Rica.
I had earned a master's degree, the Nurse Practitioner Certificate,
and was venturing into a new facet of my career.

My husband was in a similar boat. He too had a comfortable lifestyle, with a good career, and lots of personal pursuits. We enjoyed
a few years of dating, but three years later we found ourselves living
in the suburbs with a newborn in our arms, shaking our heads at

how much our lives had changed. No longer could we have sponta-neous travel plans, late-night dinners at cute little tapas restaurants, or sleep-ins on the weekend.

My husband had less time to ski and ride his motorcycle. I had less time to practice yoga, run, or cook.

While we love our children dearly, we found ourselves struggling with the balance of our individual passions and parenthood. We would have moments of mourning our "old lives" and the freedom that they had brought.

1. You did have a life before kids.

One of the first things I have learned is that it is okay to mourn your old life to a certain degree. Motherhood is a HUGE transition. While it's filled with incredible experiences like first smiles, steps, and an infinite love that you never knew existed before, it's also filled with lots of self-sacrifice.

Sometimes when things are tough, I look back at my life before kids with some envy. I have moments on the weekends when I wish I could be sleeping in or heading out to a concert without having to plan for babysitting weeks in advance. I miss drinking a coffee in solitude in the mornings rather than packing lunches and struggling to get my kids to brush their teeth. Sometimes the grass is greener and I'm just letting you know that it's okay. It doesn't make you a bad parent or a selfish individual to think about aspects of your life that you enjoyed before becoming a mother.

2. Reality check: You have changed!

With that being said though, my second piece of advice is — don't dwell on it! The reality is that you HAVE changed. You are now a MOTHER and with that comes a lot of responsibility and new demands. There's also the juggling act of figuring out who you are amidst this tremendous new role.

I think this process of figuring out who I was, was made slightly more challenging by my *advanced age*. I had my daughters when was 35 and 38 years old and had quite a bit of time to establish a lifestyle, career, and identity for myself. I had daily habits and routines that were very ingrained — for example, for years I woke up and meditated first thing in the morning.

Overall, I found that a dichotomy had formed. I was still the same woman inside, but all of the sudden I was completely distracted from my personal pursuits or too tired to engage in them. I also wasn't performing very well in the things I was doing. This really complicated that self-image I touched on. Wasn't I better than this? Who the heck was this person staring at me in the mirror? We *seasoned women* may have been used to "rocking it" in other facets of our lives. We might have climbed the corporate ladder, held high responsibility careers, managed groups of people, traveled the world, bought our own home, or built our own business. There might be a conception that if I could do all of that, why can't I do it all now? Or at least, "Why is it so hard?"

While motherhood is unbelievably fulfilling in so many ways, there was a nagging feeling in the background of, "Is this it?" I had to figure out what other aspects to myself I still NEEDED to express.

3. Carve out time for yourself to do something you really LOVE!

An important lesson I've learned (and my first step to achieving some personal sanity), was to re-prioritize my life. It sounds simple, but in fact this was one of the hardest things I had to do.

Part of the reason it was so difficult is that it meant letting go of some things that I THOUGHT were important to me to make room for things that really WERE important. For all of us, these things will be different.

For me, it involved bowing out of work commitments that extended beyond my regular workday. I started to focus on educational events that I could do during work hours (e.g., lunch and learns or conferences during the week). I also walked away from committee work that I wasn't particularly passionate about and gracefully declined a teaching position that involved long-distance travel.

I also looked at things that I really loved or were particularly important to me and put these things at the top of my list. I made sure I slotted in exercise 3x/week and a "girls' night" 2x/month. I started becoming a morning exerciser, which wouldn't be my first choice but it was the most convenient time to fit it in. I took a hard look at some of my social relationships and chose to focus on ones that really filled my cup rather than left me feeling drained.

Every Friday, I finished work at 12:00 p.m. and allocated Friday afternoons as "me" time. I gave myself permission to do whatever I wanted on this one afternoon per week. Sometimes it was a pedicure. Other times it was a workout or even a nap. I embraced the fact that carving out time for myself was in NO WAY selfish. I know that my love and affection for my daughters is no less if I choose to also nurture my individual needs.

Making these changes involved working through some feelings of guilt, but once I was able to make amends with my decisions, it fe so good to let those *distractions* go so I could focus on the things that really mattered to me. I certainly haven't mastered the art of balance, but I feel I am getting better at it day by day. I am getting better at saying NO and I'm feeling less and less regretful about it.

Time is SO precious for all of us. It's important to figure out what truly makes you happy in order to create a life that allows you to be the best mother and woman you can be. Make sure that when you carve time out for yourself that it's for something that you truly LOVE, as opposed to something you feel obligated to do.

4. Let go of preconceived notions or expectations.

I know for me, placing high and often unrealistic expectations on myself also created a lot of unnecessary anxiety and stress. From this, I have learned a few key things. Let go of any expectations or preconceived notions you have for yourself as an individual and as a mother.

The first few years of motherhood are pretty messy as we are all trying to figure things out. Children are unpredictable and will throw curveballs at you every day. Some days will feel manageable, while other days you might feel like cracking a bottle of wine at 9:00 a.m. Give yourself permission to be less than perfect and not always in control. It's okay to cry and feel frustrated. We all have those moments, trust me!

Also, remember that motherhood is a marathon, not a sprint. It takes a while to get your footing but, over time, you learn new hacks to make your life a little easier. I now have a rule of no snacks in the car (outside of road trips of course!) because quite frankly I was tired of vacuuming the car seats every week. I have also become stricter about screen time because I know my children behave poorly on the days they have more television. You will figure out what works for you!

5. Ask for help and build a supportive group of mom friends.

Finally, don't be afraid to enlist the help of others. One benefit of having kids at a later stage in life is that the grandparents might be retired and have a little more free time! If not, it might come down to off-setting with your partner or enlisting babysitters or friends.

To all the single mothers out there — I bow to you and this network of support might be even bigger! I used to feel weak at the idea of asking for help. I think this stemmed from having a demanding career and valuing my capabilities. Asking for help made me feel like a failure; as though motherhood had gotten the better of me. Enlisting a strong and supportive group of *mom friends* was one of the best things that I ever did. I found particular solace in women around my own age, with similar life experiences. These women helped me to work through these feelings of defeat. Being able to share our mutual experiences and struggles was so cathartic. I loved the frankness of my *seasoned* mom friends. I could completely be myself and open up about the struggles without any fear of judgment.

One friend openly shared her experience of postpartum anxiety (something I've never had the courage to do) and it made me feel such a strong connection to her. I had a tremendous amount of anxiety after the birth of both of my daughters and her story became a catalyst for me to start working through my own mental health struggles. Mom friends are also great problem solvers! From diaper rashes to discipline, to ramping up your sex life — with mom friends, nothing is off limits!

All the life experience that I have gained as a woman of *advanced maternal age*, I've come to learn, is actually a real gift. While I mourn the loss of my freedom from time to time, I also look at the experiences I have and think about the wisdom and knowledge that I can pass down to my daughters. The truth is, we have all done so much and have valuable wisdom to share.

For us *seasoned* women, shifting the focus from what has been taken away to what we can give has helped me work through some of the confusion that I have felt in my new role as a mother. It might take some re-prioritizing or enlisting the help of others, but it is possible to strike the balance we need. I now look at my age and experience as valuable assets, rather than limitations, and it provides me with the confidence to know that I CAN rock this mom thing!

References

1. Lampinen, Vehvilainen and Kankkunen (2009). "A Review of Pregnancy in Women Over 35 Years of Age." Open Nurse Journal. 3: 33–38.

Key Takeaway

Reflect on this author's work and write down one key idea, concept, or theme that you can take with you in your own life! If something really hit home, connect with the author and get social!

Chapter 31
Jessica Minicola

Author Photo: Cayley Black Photography
Find Jessica: @jessicaminicola

My name is Jessica Minicola. I am a mother and step-mother to four beautiful children and a life-learner. I believe in enjoying the little moments in life because it is over before you know it. I founded a passion project of mine called On The Flip in 2018. The mission is to bring awareness around consumer purchases and to provide sustainable options for buyers. In 2019, I founded the Mamas for Mamas Kitchener-Waterloo charity branch where the mission is to ensure that no mama or child is ever left behind. I want to thank my children and my parents for guiding me into the person I am today. I would not be who I am today if it wasn't for you.

***

Motherhood began for me when I stepped into the role of a stepmom (also known as a bonus mom) when I was 25 years old. I instantly became a "mom" to three children who were two, four, and 12. In 2017, my hubby and I blended our family with our son. I have been lucky enough to be able to mother both biological and non-biological children. Motherhood revolutionized my life. It is like no endeavour I have ever journeyed, so cliché, I know! The journey of motherhood reshaped me into a Jessica 2.0. It showed me that we are never done learning our emotions. It taught me the importance of self-care, daily routine, adaptability, and most importantly, that being a mother is a gift.

1. Emotions

As all kids set their own rhythm, so do we as mamas. We beat to the rhythm of life based on our emotions and our emotional state. I have learned through motherhood, that when we can embody our emotions and learn to process them, we can respond and show up to life with a positive mindset and perspective, not only for ourselves but for our babies. One of my favourite ways to process my emotions is through song and dance. It breaks my mood and adds humour. I want to believe it is one of my kids' favourite things to watch me do. The neat thing about processing my emotions is it helps me to respond versus react.

2. Self-care

Self-care is not selfish. I have learned to let go of the shame that fills moms with mom guilt. Repeat this mantra with me:

I am not a bad mom.
I can take personal time
— and enjoy it.
Let this time transcend me into
the strong, caring mama that I am.

The quicker we can work through our emotions that self-care is not selfish and that everyone will survive and adapt, the easier it is to be authentically happy.

When I processed my emotions around self-care, I realized how much I was lacking in confidence and the values I held. I asked myself, "How am I supposed to teach my kids values and integrity if I don't have strong values for myself?" By recognizing what I need for self-care, I was able to re-develop my values, boundaries, and in the end — my identity. Without self-care, I would be walking around feeling overwhelmed, frustrated, and most likely on the verge of a breakdown, serving nobody. Personal time allows you to fill your cup so you can pour your positive vibes into and onto your family. Remember, you can only do what you can do and that will look different for everyone. Do not compare yourself to others.

3. Routine

Routine assists emotional, cognitive, and social development. It relieves a lot of stress and frustration. I have come to learn that, as a family, we need a routine for our mental health. There were times when we fell out of our daily routines, such as when a global pandemic sent us into lockdown. I quickly noticed that not only do I depend deeply on a routine to keep me feeling good as a mama, but my children also depend on the routine in order to keep them happy.

As a mom, I was feeling frustrated that the kids were not listening to me; the kids were feeling frustrated, which caused more chaos. That is when I had an ah-ha moment. I need to model the behaviour I want to see in my children. Writing this, I feel silly. Nonetheless, this has been a big lesson in our family. We have learned that our children are truly watching and observing our actions.

I have found when I do not have a set and thoughtfully planned out routine my children are wild animals. Without a routine, they do not know what the expectations are and are directionless. With routine, they complain and drag their feet but I know in time the routine will be of value and it makes them feel safe. The healthy habits that will be programmed into their subconscious will empower them to make healthy choices.

4. Adaptability

Motherhood is a fine balancing act. You are balancing your well-being and your children's well-being and it can be a lot. I have found that letting go of my expectations and being more adaptable has been my saving grace. It took me being pulled in a hundred directions, feeling overwhelmed and unbalanced, to realize that I need to pick my battles and become a bit more adaptable to the requests of my littles. I have learned that being adaptable allows my kids to have "authority" and feel in control of their decisions (for the most part). It is my goal to honour my children's uniqueness without my beliefs and ideologies influencing them. I want to make it clear that I am not perfect and will always be striving toward my goals.

5. Blessing

Motherhood can be hard emotionally and physically. It literally changes you physically and mentally. That is why there is the great saying, "It takes a village." I have learned especially during 2020 that change is the one thing that is constant in life and with change comes the process of adaptation. We change and then we adapt. The quicker we can learn to adapt, the quicker we teach our littles to adapt. The quicker we can work through our emotions, the quicker our littles can learn how to work through theirs. I have taken motherhood as a way of relearning. It is a never-ending journey of learning. I educate and research to learn how to be adaptive. It is not something that comes naturally and easily. It takes work and time.

The common thread I see between the five lessons I have learned through motherhood is that they all hold wisdom, love, vulnerability, and grit. When we, on a collective basis, can understand the normal emotions of motherhood, we can be kinder to ourselves and each other.

Motherhood is not a race.

It is not about who can do it better.

It is about being ourselves and doing our best.

Key Takeaway

Reflect on this author's work and write down one key idea, concept, or theme that you can take with you in your own life! If something really hit home, connect with the author and get social!

Chapter 32

Taylin Lee

Author Photo: Alexis Burton Photography
Find Taylin: @taylin.leee

Putting all the lessons I have learned through motherhood into one chapter is a near-impossible task. I guess I would start by saying that motherhood is everything I had hoped for. I have experienced things that I never expected and have felt a world of emotions and thoughts that I didn't know existed. It is a task that you can never prepare for and a chapter of one's life that I don't think we can ever be truly ready for.

Motherhood has rocked me, challenged me, and changed me in ways I never thought possible! Yet, it has opened my heart and showed me unconditional love stronger than I knew possible.

In my chapter, I hope to sum up some of what I feel are the nec

essary survival tools for motherhood. I will warn anyone considering becoming a parent though, that even when you think you are
ready... you aren't. To be a parent is to feel powerless and vulnerable
while falling so very deeply in love with another human at the same
time. You would sacrifice your whole being to watch them sleep.
Take these so-called lessons with a grain of salt as they are merely
my perspective. Mama (aka YOU!) always knows what's best for her
baby.

1. Mama knows best.

Diaper brand, bottle or breast, co-sleeping, crib and then cry it out
method are only a few of the hundreds of choices you will be faced
with as a new parent. Whether you ask for advice when it comes to
your new baby or not, trust me when I say that it will be given. Hundreds and maybe even thousands of times throughout your child's
life you will be told how best to care for your child. Doctors, mothers,
fathers-in-law, parents, siblings, friends, and even random strangers on the street will feel entitled enough to let you know what they
think is best for your child.

There are several ways that you can handle this (often unsolicited)
advice. You can smile while letting it pass in one ear and out the other; you can take it to heart and be hard on yourself; or, you can argue
your own opinion. In my experience, the solution for this common
parenthood problem is simply to reply with, "Wow that's an interesting perspective! As my child's mother, I know them best, so I will
keep loving them in whichever way feels right for us."

What you're doing is acknowledging their suggestions without
agreeing or disagreeing with them. You are simply letting them
know that you are confident in your ability to take care of your baby.
Here is the thing though. No doctor, parent, or friend in this world
knows your baby like you. No one else has watched that tiny human

breathe while sleeping. No one else can distinguish their ten different cries. The first — and I feel, the most important — lesson in motherhood is to simply know that you, as their mom, will always know what's best.

2. Your child isn't bad. They are human.

Can you imagine if every time you had a bad day, an anxious day, a tired and grumpy day — that people decided that this incident made you a bad person? It would be irrational to label an adult as bad or less than, merely based on one day's particularly difficult mood. Which is why I always find it interesting how quickly babies and small children can be labeled as bad for simply doing what we as humans all do.

They don't get spa days, they don't get counseling appointments, tea with their best friend, or even the ability to understand and communicate their feelings on a bad day. Yet we have this expectation of our children to always behave and "be good!" In your darkest moments (and I promise you will have them) when your child will not sleep, when they have shouted "NO!" for the tenth time that morning, I urge you instead of thinking or saying "why do you have to be so bad?" instead say, "I am sorry you are having such a tough moment."

Then hug that beautiful vulnerable child, give yourself a break, breathe and start over. The sooner you learn to accept your child for the not-always-perfect, beautiful person that they are, the sooner your expectation of yourself as the perfect parent of a perfectly behaved child will diminish. And your need to always have things be calm will come to a stop.

3. Those who mind don't matter and those who matter don't mind.

There will come a moment in parenthood when your child will decide at a moment's notice to make what we refer to as a "scene." Trust me when I say: your beautiful child will pick the most public and inappropriate moment, usually when you are already exhausted, to have a fit. In this moment, I urge you to remember that we have all been there. And when the other mothers in the store look over, what they are probably not thinking is "Wow! What a bad mom." Instead, they are most likely thinking, "Oh man! I've been there!" You will feel your face go red and you will want to grab your child and run for the car. However, try not to be so hard on yourself or your child. Instead, take a deep breath and dig deep to find your sense of humour.

Remember, we have all been there and if we haven't, then we haven't had children yet. This is one of the many adventures of parenthood! The negative reactions of those around you has little to do with your abilities and more to do with their lack of understanding. Put a smile on, Mama. Look for the humour in it, and hold your head high as you pull your screaming child into the next aisle.

4. Your child knows what they need.

I'm talking about an unfinished plate of food, untaken cold medicine, or maybe a skipped nap. Many times throughout your child's life, they will refuse something. They will yell, scream, and stomp their feet. They may cry ... and maybe you will cry too. You are mom, after all, and you know what your child needs.

Now, although in lesson one I told you that mama always knows best, there is one occasion where someone *jusssst* maybe might know better than you, and that is your child. I would like to share a story a good friend once told me.

Her son was sick with a cold and he always refused cold medicine because he said it made him sick. My friend assumed that she knew what her son needed. She secretly crushed up the three tablets of medicine and put them in his shake. A few minutes after having the shake her son said, "Mommy, I don't feel well. Was there medicine in that shake?" My friend has assured me that there was no way her then 7-year-old could have known about her secret except that he knows how medicine makes him feel. The tough lesson my friend learned that day was to always honour your child.

I can't count the number of times I have begged, pleaded, and cried for my child to nap assuming that because it is 12:00 p.m., it must be time to nap. What I have come to learn is that my daughter knows her body. Maybe that night she slept well, maybe that day she played less. But for whatever reason, today's nap wasn't necessary. The battle to make your child do what you want them to do with their body is a lost cause. I have come to find that the best solution is to say, "Okay, baby, maybe we will try again later." Maybe the nap comes, maybe it doesn't. But I will promise you one thing, you might just avoid having a twenty-minute fight and many tears to go along with it.

5. You are more than just a mother.

Whether you are trying to get pregnant, are pregnant, are in the process of adopting or becoming a mom to a partner with children you will inevitably encounter sacrifice. Every time you give up that glass of wine, night out, or savings for something that you wanted for yourself, you will change in some small way. These sacrifices wi feel like the easiest ones to make because they are for the sake of someone you love so deeply.

While being a parent is all about sacrifice, I feel it's important to re-member that you don't need to lose yourself to be deemed a great parent. You can return to work, gather with friends, drink an extra glass of wine, sleep in on Sunday, and still be the most bomb parent on the planet. You have to put your oxygen mask on first in order to be the most incredible parent. Self-love must be a factor that you prioritize.

So, remember to take the job, enjoy the party, and allow the babysitter to come over. Loving yourself doesn't mean that you love your child any less. It means that you love them enough to take care of YOU, to be your best for THEM.

Key Takeaway

Reflect on this author's work and write down one key idea,
concept, or theme that you can take with you in your own life! If
something really hit home, connect with the author and get social!

....
....
....
....
....
....
....
....
....
....
....
....
....
....
....
....
....
....

Epilogue

Courtney StCroix

I really feel like I'm doing a disservice to life if I'm not extracting lessons from every corner of my experiences. We start out spending a vast majority of our lives in a learning phase; from day one, we're taking in everything around us and learning about how we fit in to this big world (with the help of our mothers, of course!). We spend years in the school system, learning everything we can, getting regularly tested and challenged, and understanding that some subjects we like more than others; some lessons are easier to absorb than others. We're accustomed to having textbooks and workbooks and homework, and there's a clearly laid out curriculum guiding us through what we're "supposed to" know at any given stage.

And then? Somehow, we become adults who are bearing our own children and suddenly ... there are no designated, approved learning tools to support our growth. There aren't any motherhood textbooks. There's no designated and age-specific teacher guiding you through every new year of parenthood. There are no parenting degrees, programs, or certifications that, when complete, prepare you perfectly for the longest job you'll ever have in your life. The things that we grew up leaning on through our learning experiences aren't really there. There are no parent police, there aren't any quizzes or tests to check your knowledge, and there are no predictable scenarios. There's just trial and error, a lot of dirty diapers filled with a lot of human feces, endless snack-making, responding the best you can to a divinely unique human behaving in divinely unique ways, life and work balancing acts, personality molding and learning how to both parent and teach our children to be good humans at the same time.

There's no easy answer to motherhood, just *lessons*. Absorb the lessons, especially the hard ones. Your motherhood experience is so incredibly different from mine, from your best friend's, and from your own mother's. There are tough lessons, challenges, and hard climbs, and there are beautiful teachable moments between parent and child. There is physical growth as your children expand before your eyes, jumping clothing sizes at impossible rates ... and there is palpable mental and emotional growth as you learn how to overcome the hard parts and build on the strong woman and mother you've been all along.

There are no textbooks, but if you look around hard enough, you'll be able to find in your fellow parents the mentors and guides you maybe didn't think were there. Nobody is qualified to give advice, but we're all welcome to share our experiences. We're all available to listen. We're all here for connection. And we're all able to tell our story. And that may just be the best teacher there is.

Live your life in a way that allows you to extract the lessons from every experience. I promise, you will not regret any opportunity to learn. And our kids — they're here to guide us through leaps of our own that we never knew were possible.

Here's to motherhood, and all the lessons we're learning together.

Cheers, Mama!
Courtney

Other books available from

For more information on books, publishing and co authoring, visit

LEAD-HER.COM